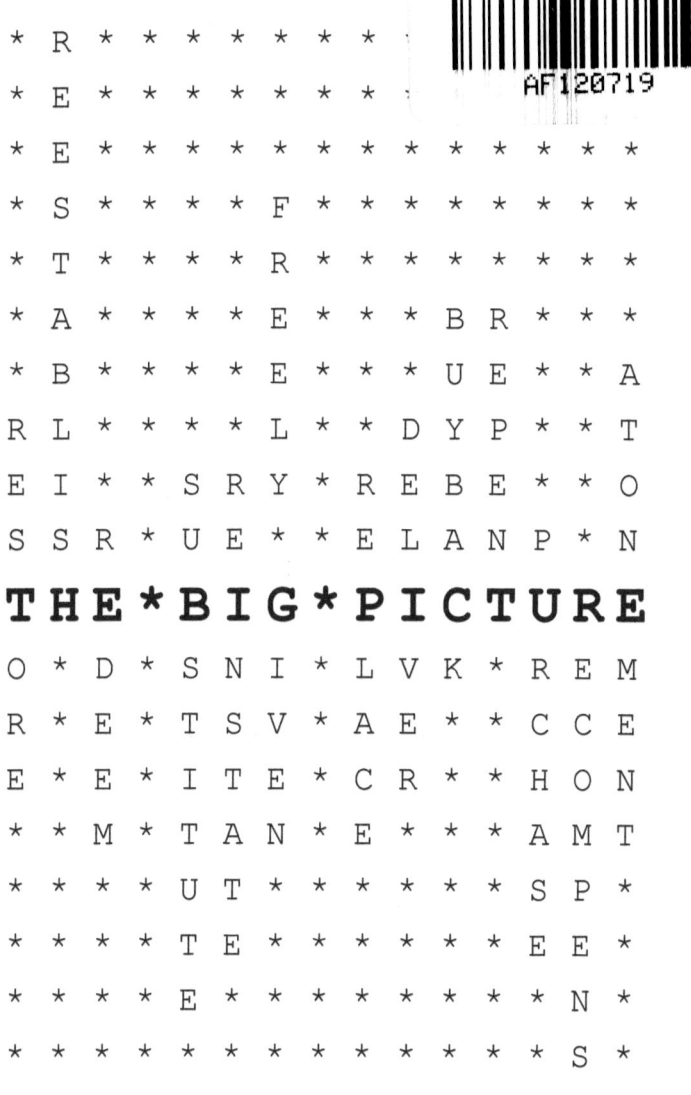

THE *BIG* PICTURE

Beyr Reyes, PhD

THE BIG PICTURE

Beyr Reyes, PhD
Copyright @ 2008 ShadeTree Publishing, LLC
Print ISBN 978-0-9822632-0-4
e-Book ISBN: 978-0-9822632-1-1

Scripture quotations marked "NIV" are taken from the HOLY BIBLE, NEW INTERNATIONAL VERSION®. Copyright © 1973, 1978, 1984 International Bible Society. Used by permission of Zondervan. All rights reserved.

Scripture quotations marked "NKJV" are taken from the New King James Version®. Copyright © 1982 by Thomas Nelson, Inc. All rights reserved.

Scripture quotations marked "KJV" are taken from the King James Version. The KJV is public domain in the United States.

All rights reserved. This book is protected by copyright. No part of this book may be reproduced or transmitted in any form or by any means, electronic or mechanical, including photocopying, recording, or by any information storage and retrieval system, without permission in writing from the publisher.

The purpose of this book is to educate and enlighten. This book is sold with the understanding that the author and publisher are not engaged in rendering counseling, albeit it professional or lay, to the reader or anyone else. The author and publisher shall have neither liability nor responsibility to any person or entity with respect to any loss or damage caused, or alleged to have been caused, directly or indirectly, by the information contained in this book.

Visit our Web site at www.ShadeTreePublishing.com.

Contents

PREFACE	1
Chapter 1 INTRODUCTION	3
Chapter 2 CREATION AND THE FALL OF MAN	7
Chapter 3 GOD'S REDEMPTION PLAN	17
Chapter 4 IMPORTANT COVENANTS	21
Chapter 5 NEW COVENANT	31
Chapter 6 SATAN'S PLAN	41
Chapter 7 IN THE END	55
Chapter 8 THE BIG PICTURE IN A NUTSHELL	82
Chapter 9 MAKE A CHOICE	98
ABOUT THE AUTHOR	102
OTHER BOOKS BY BEYR REYES	104
ACKNOWLEDGEMENTS	110
REVIEW REQUEST	112
REFERENCES	114

First and foremost, this book is dedicated to the Lord. He inspired it; His Word is the source for its existence.

I would also like to dedicate this book to my darling David and my beautiful Julia. They both are gifts from God straight to my heart.

To my Mother, I send my love and respect, and certainly thanks for being a wonderful parent and friend.

To Linda Morris, I offer my deepest gratitude for her unending perseverance of shining the light of the Redeemer for those in the dark.

And to a special friend who inspired me to complete this book—may it speak to her spirit.

PREFACE

April 23, 2008, in a Wednesday night class at Church, this book hit me like a Mack truck. The ideas and concepts flooded my mind as I feverously jotted down everything I could. My fingers and thoughts had never before worked so smoothly and efficiently together. Later that night, I outlined the entire book and added a large amount of the text. I have no doubt that this book was inspired by God. It's delivery to my mind and hand was Divine.

Most folks know the stories about Creation, the Jewish nation, and Jesus, but they don't know how all these things are connected. Furthermore, when it comes to reading the Bible, there are several types of people: 1) those who never read it for themselves; 2) those who read it but get frustrated because they don't understand it and then quit; 3) those who read it and can't tell you a thing they've read but continue to read anyway; and 4) those who dive into the scriptures and look for hidden spiritual truths and prophesies. This book is written for all these people. It is a broad perspective of the Bible that will help the beginner to place events and their purposes. For the reader who always has his or her head buried in certain passages, this book is a refreshing step back to help illuminate the big picture.

However, if you're the type of person who needs heart-touching stories or miraculous anecdotes to keep you interested, this book isn't for you. In fact, this book isn't for the faint-hearted. It is loaded with scripture and facts that only a seeker of truth and wisdom would appreciate. If you're a person who is looking for deeper knowledge and a broader understanding—a person who doesn't need the fluff and unlike an infant, prefers meat to milk—then read on, my friend.

Chapter 1
INTRODUCTION

God has a plan. It's just that simple.

"For I know the plans I have for you," declares the Lord. (Jer. 29:11 NIV)

As the Psalmists so eloquently put it:

Many, O Lord my God, are the wonders you have done. The things you planned for us no one can recount to you; were I to speak and tell of them, they would be too many to declare. (Ps. 40:5 NIV)

O Lord, you are my God; I will exalt you and praise your name, for in perfect faithfulness you have done marvelous things, things planned long ago. (Is. 25:1 NIV)

Knowing the beginning from the end, God made plans to prosper us and not to harm us, plans to give us hope and a future. Even more, God has something better for us, so that only together with us, will His promises be made perfect.

God's marvelous plan for us is revealed in scripture. He does nothing without revealing His plan to his servants the prophets. He makes known to us the mystery of His will according to His good pleasure, to be put into effect when the times reach their fulfillment.

All of creation waits in eager expectation for God's plans to be revealed. However, it is our human nature to be impatient. The Lord warns us about such behavior:

> [Woe] *to those who say, "Let God hurry, let him hasten his work so we may see it. Let it approach, let the plan of the Holy One of Israel come, so we may know it."* (Is. 5:19 NIV)

The Lord tells us that we are to seek His plans for us. He says that it is the glory of God to conceal a matter, and to search out a matter is the glory of kings. In addition, we are to set our minds on things above, not on earthly things. We are to look for His will and not ours.

However, oftentimes we cannot comprehend God's plan in its entirety. We don't always know the thoughts of the Lord and we don't understand His plan. His thoughts are above our thoughts, and His ways are above our ways.

God also warns us about losing sight of God's will for our life and implementing our own plans:

> *"Woe to the obstinate children,"* declares the Lord, *"to those who carry out plans that are not mine, forming an alliance, but not by my Spirit, heaping sin upon sin."* (Is. 30:1 NIV)

The plans in our hearts are many. Nevertheless, it is the Lord's purpose that will prevail. Although a man may plan his course, the Lord determines his steps. This isn't to say that everything is the Lord's fault. We certainly have free will and exercise it regularly in sinful matters. (We can't blame the Lord for our poor choices.)

God's plan is unconditional. If God says it will happen, then rest assured that it will come to pass. The plans of the Lord stand firm forever and through all generations. The Lord Almighty has sworn that surely as He has planned, it will be. He says that His word will go forth from His mouth, will not return void, will accomplish what He pleases, and will prosper. There is no wisdom, no insight, or no plan that can succeed against the Lord.

Beyr Reyes

Chapter 2
CREATION AND THE FALL OF MAN

Before creation, there was God. God has always been, always is, and always will be. From everlasting to everlasting, He is God. He is omniscient (all knowing), omnipresent (everywhere at all times), and omnipotent (all powerful). He knew the fate of the world before He ever created it. So why then did He do it?

God wants fellowship. The Bible states that He called us into fellowship, and it is so important to God that He instituted a special offering for it–the fellowship offering. Before creation, God had the angels and heavenly hosts for companionship. Why then would He want or need fellowship with man?

If you had a choice to spend time with something, to walk and talk with it, what would you choose? A gerbil? A cricket? A leaf? The sidewalk? Of course, you would choose another human being. Preferably someone with whom you would have things in common. God made Adam, a living being with whom He could fellowship and linger in the garden.

With His words, God first spoke the world into existence. Once God had prepared a suitable place for man,

He created Adam. He formed the man from the dust of the ground and breathed into his nostrils the breath of life, and the man became a living being. God didn't speak us into existence, but rather, took the dust of the ground to mold and shape and breathed our life into us. The creation of man was intimate. Then as His final creation, woman was made from the rib of Adam. She was the only thing created from another living being. Some folks believe that the creation of Eve was the grand finale of all God's creation.

God created man (mankind) in His own image. What does it mean to be created in the image of God? Perhaps he had heavenly power and even the ability to create. But what Adam had, that was unlike God, was corruptibility. Adam lacked perfection and purity.

In addition to companionship reasons, perhaps God thought that Adam possessed too much power for one human to handle. (Okay—this thought and the following rationale are entirely supposition, but interesting to ponder.). What if He split off Eve from Adam, thereby creating two human beings that together as one, possessed the power initially created? Adam and Eve, as husband and wife, could only wield the power when they came together as one (for example, to create another human being—however, God breathes the living breath into the flesh). In Genesis, the Bible states that a man will leave his father and mother and be united to his wife, and they will become one flesh. Jesus said, "So they are no longer two, but one. Therefore, what God has joined together, let man not separate."[1] Jesus also said that when two on earth agree about anything they ask for, it will be done. Any prayerful husband and wife have witnessed this.

THE BIG PICTURE

God chose us before the creation of the world to be holy and blameless in His sight. In love, He predestined us to be adopted as His sons. God is pure and powerful, and we were created in His likeness. However, like the fallen angels, our power and purity are corruptible.

Of course, before creation, God could foresee the fall of man. After all, look what happened with one third of the angels that fell from Heaven. How much harder and farther would man fall? God knew the consequences of creating man, but He had a master plan right from the start.

The Lord took man and put him in the Garden of Eden to work it and to take care of it. Then God said, "Let them rule over the fish of the sea and the birds of the air, over the livestock, over all the earth, and over all the creatures that move along the ground."2 God blessed Adam and Eve and said to them, "Be fruitful and increase in number; fill the earth and subdue it."3

In the garden, God walked with Adam in the cool of the day. God had the fellowship He wanted, and He made sure that Adam and Eve had everything they wanted too. God said, "I give you every seed-bearing plant on the face of the whole earth and every tree that has fruit with seed in it. They will be yours for food. And to all the beasts of the earth and all the birds of the air and all the creatures that move on the ground—everything that has the breath of life in it— I give every green plant for food."4

God told Adam and Eve that they could eat everything of the Garden except for the fruit from one particular tree— the Tree of Knowledge of Good and Evil. He commanded the man, saying, "Of every tree of the Garden thou may freely eat. But of the tree of the knowledge of good and evil, thou shalt not eat of it: for in the day that thou eat thereof thou shalt surely die."5

Why did God place the forbidden tree in the Garden if He knew it would cause man to die? God is omniscient. He knew that the tree would cause Adam and Eve to sin and fall from paradise. Why then did He put it there if things were already going so great?

The tree was a means for man to gain knowledge about good and evil. Perhaps (again, supposition) God had not created man to have this knowledge from the start because man would have had both knowledge *and* power, yet would have still been corruptible. Knowledge + power + corruptibility equals a formidable combination! Man needed to be purified of this corruptibleness before he could be given full power. Therefore, not only would the tree have been a means of gaining knowledge, but also the beginning of the way to purification of man. God arranged it so that the acquisition of knowledge occurred at the same time as the purification process. When Adam and Eve ate from the forbidden Tree of Knowledge of Good and Evil, they gained knowledge, and at the same time, they brought about the first sin upon mankind.

****

A similar question heard before is: Why did God give Adam and Eve the rule about eating from the tree if He already knew that they would break it?

First of all, without a command, there is no choice. Presumably, God didn't want robots. In addition, if you tell someone to not do something, it is likely they will inevitably turn around and do it. Every parent knows this, especially our Heavenly Father. The battle with sin had not come into the world yet, but something else had—temptation. Satan was in the world and ready to take down man.

When God spoke aloud the rule in the garden, Adam and Eve were not the only ones who heard it. Satan was most certainly listening too, and God was probably counting on this. God knew that in Satan's jealousy of man's relationship with God, Satan could not resist initiating strife. Little did Satan know that his creator not only could foresee his actions, but also could read his heart. Even Satan had a roll in God's master plan. God gave Adam and Eve the rule about the forbidden tree because they had to do something out of disobedience in order to bring about sin and the resulting purification of man.

Now we know why God would have put the tree in the garden. But why did Adam and Eve eat from it, if they already had everything they wanted? The Bible answers this question too. It says that the serpent was more cunning than any beast of the field. Satan asked Eve, "Has God indeed said, 'You shall not eat of every tree of the garden?'"6 Basically, Satan was asking: Did God *really* say this? Are you sure? The enemy placed doubt in Eve's mind and effectively separated her from God. As a side note, isn't this what the enemy always tries to do to man? Trying to steal the promises of God from us and to make us doubt God's word?

The serpent also tried to make the situation sound worse than it really was. He asked about eating from *every* tree (some translations say *any* tree). He made it sound like Adam and Eve were very limited in what they could do. This is another arrow in the enemy's quiver for his attack against us. Satan can make us think that being a Christian is all about rules and not getting to have fun and be free. Lies, all lies.

It is evident by Eve's reaction that the serpent's comment struck a nerve. She immediately sets him straight by telling him that they *may* eat the fruit from the trees in the garden. Then she clarifies God's rule by telling the serpent that they will surely die if they eat from *the* tree in the middle of the garden.

Then the serpent said to Eve, "You will not surely die."7 Can't you just hear the serpent's poisonous tone as he casually dismisses God's words and sows dissent? Satan was deceiving Eve by making her question why God would create her then let her die. The enemy was trying to make God look like a liar, or like God was exaggerating the punishment and didn't mean what He said.

Satan went on to further mislead Eve. He told her that the reason God didn't want them to eat from the tree was because it would open their eyes make them know evil. This part was true; however, Satan went on to weave lies into the fabric of the truth. He told them that they would become gods too if they ate from the tree.

> *And the serpent said unto the woman, ye shall not surely die: For God doth know that in the day ye eat thereof, then your eyes shall be opened, and ye shall be as gods, knowing good and evil.* (Gen. 3:4-5 KJV)

When the woman saw that the fruit of the tree was good for food and pleasing to the eye, and also desirable for gaining wisdom, she took some and ate it. She also gave some to her husband, who was with her, and he ate it. *Then* the eyes of both of them were opened. Both Adam *and* Eve ate the fruit before the fall of man came about. Some people believe that man didn't fall until Adam ate from the tree because he was the one whom God instructed. If this were the case, then Eve would have been, and would continue to be, free from the curse of sin and death. As we know, Eve was and is accountable.

Adam and Eve took the fruit because they fell for the devil's tricks. Satan used (and still uses today) many techniques to separate man from God. He made them doubt God's word, he made them think that God doesn't mean what He says, and he convinced them that they could be gods too (basic humanism that runs rampant today).

Once Adam and Eve ate from the forbidden tree, God's master plan shifted into high gear. When they performed this first act of disobedience, sin was created and death was born. Man became corrupted; man now had knowledge of power, but was drenched in sin. Adam and Eve had to leave the Garden. They could no longer reside there and linger in the company of God. From this point on, man could only come to God through the priests in the temple.

In the temple, there was a curtain separating the Holy Place from the Most Holy Place (also known as the Holy of Holies). Inside the Most Holy Place was the Ark of the Covenant containing the tablets of the Commandments, the Rod of Aaron, and a pot of manna. Upon this Ark (His Mercy Seat), sat the Almighty. Man was sinful and could not approach God directly. Only the High Priest could step behind the curtain and into God's presence. The high priest was the only one who could enter the Most Holy Place after a plethora of sacrifices and rituals; he had to purify himself before entering or he would drop dead. God would not tolerate sin in His presence.

Another reason Adam and Eve were evicted from the Garden was because God didn't want them to live forever in their sinful state. He removed them from the Garden so they could no longer eat from the tree of life, and thus live eternally in sin.

> And the Lord God said, "The man has now become like one of us, knowing good and evil. He must not be allowed to reach out his hand and take also from the tree of life and eat, and live forever." So the Lord God banished him from the Garden of Eden to work the ground from which he had been taken. After he drove the man out, he placed on the east side of the Garden of Eden cherubim and a flaming sword flashing back and forth to guard the way to the tree of life. (Gen. 3:22-24 NIV)

Adam and Eve lost their anointing and power. They were stripped spiritually. As they stood naked in flesh and spirit, they became aware of their exposure and vulnerability. God slew the first sacrificial animal to cover the nakedness of Adam and Eve, both physically and spiritually.

Adam lost much, including his position as ruler and caretaker of the garden. It is important to note that Adam was not the owner of the earth and all it contained. God was and still is the owner; the earth is the Lord's and the fullness thereof. Adam was simply a steward, someone to take care of the earth for the Lord. Although Adam was given the right to rule the earth, he was not given the title Ruler. When Adam and Eve sinned against God, they forfeited their blessing from God and the position of man as the lord of creation. Adam lost his rights to Satan, and Satan gained dominion over the earth. It was given unto him to make war with the saints, and to overcome them, and power was given him over all families, tongues, and nations.

Man lost more than his ruling rights, though. He, in fact, lost his very life. When man fell into sin, he fell to his death (not just death of flesh, but death of the soul—a finality of existence). Death *is* the wages of sin, and the Scripture declares that the whole world is a prisoner of sin. Sin is crouching at your door. It desires to have you.

> *"Hell from beneath is excited about you, to meet you at your coming; it stirs up the dead for you, all the chief ones of the earth; it has raised up from their thrones all the kings of the nations. They all shall speak and say to you: 'Have you also become as weak as we? Have you become like us? Your pomp is brought down to Sheol, and the sound of your stringed instruments; the maggot is spread under you, and worms cover you.'"* (Is. 14:9-11 NKJV)

Sin is nothing more than disobedience of God, and man is born into the original sin of Adam. Therefore, without a savior, we are doomed to death.

Chapter 3
GOD'S REDEMPTION PLAN

Why didn't God make us perfect like He wanted from the beginning? Why did man have to go through all this? The fact is that God *did* make us like He wanted us to be; He made us in His image.

If God would have made us perfect from the beginning, He would have simply made Himself. God is perfect, without blemish. He is pure and holy. Anything short of this is corruptible in nature. Anything like this is God Himself.

God had a plan. He chose us, before the creation of the world, to be holy and blameless in His sight. However, like the fallen angels, our power and purity were corruptible. Once man fell, he was forever steeped in sin and thus separated from the holiness of God. With this advent of sin, death gained the right to man's life. The Bible says that the wages of sin is death. Not only would man struggle in this new existence, but because Adam (by commission of sin) abdicated his dominion over the earth, man would become subject to Satan and his demonic principalities. Man would forever wrestle with sinful temptations and battle with death. Caught in this viscous cycle of sin and death, man would appear to have no hope.

From this, God's heart was broken. After all, He created man as a companion but was now separated from him. Furthermore, His heart ached when He saw His children suffering and crying out for help. God wanted to bring man back to Him. But to do so, God first had to find a way around sin and death. He had to make sure that man was sinless if he were destined to live forever with Him. If there were some way that sin could be removed from man, then man could live with God forever. God's plan involved redemption.

According to The American Heritage® Dictionary of the English Language,8 the definition of <u>redeem</u> is

* *To recover ownership of by paying a specified sum.
* *To pay off (a promissory note, for example).
* *To turn in and receive something in exchange.
* *To fulfill (a pledge, for example).
* *To set free; rescue or ransom.
* *To save from a state of sinfulness and its consequences.
* *To make up for.
* *To restore the honor, worth, or reputation of.

Redemption is the act of being redeemed.

God began to formulate a long-term plan to bring about man's redemption. He needed a single blood sacrifice to ultimately cover all of mankind. Because the plan would take some time to unfold, God offered a temporary solution of animal sacrifices.

The Bible says that life is in the blood. Therefore, if man's sin could be placed on another living creature, the sacrifice of that creature and the shedding of its blood would cover the sin and temporarily bring life to man. The creature would die with the sin. Death would accept the creature's life (blood) as payment.

Animal blood for atonement was really only a postponement. The sin was covered, but not removed. There is a difference: covering means that although it cannot be seen, it is still there. The interim redemption plan worked for removing sin temporarily; however, death still had a right to man, and make no mistake, it came for man regularly. Even though someone may have just offered a sacrifice for the atonement of his sin, as soon as he walked away, the sin meter started ticking again. This is because we continually carry the original sin of Adam and Eve.

God needed to send man a sacrifice that could permanently blot out sin and conquer death. Mankind needed a savior. Job may not have completely known and understood God, but he did understand the need for this savior. He knew that he needed someone able to stand before the throne and plead his case. He said, "If only there were someone to arbitrate between us."[9] Someone to say, "Deliver him from going down to the pit, I have found a ransom."[10]

Job also knew that this savior already existed. He said, "Even now my witness is in Heaven; my advocate is on high. My intercessor is my friend."[11] He went on to say, "I know my redeemer lives and that in the end he will stand upon the earth."[12]

The prophets spoke much about the coming savior, the Redeemer. The prophet Isaiah spoke more about the Redeemer than anyone else. Chapter 53 of Isaiah speaks of specific details about Him. In Chapter 59, the Lord said[13]: "And the Redeemer shall come to Zion, and unto them that turn from transgression in Jacob." Other Old Testament prophets, including Daniel, Micah, Zechariah, and Malachi, foretold of details about the Redeemer and His ministry.

****

God had a plan, and He recorded it for us in scripture. His plan would involve the Redeemer, who would take away the sin of man.

Chapter 4
IMPORTANT COVENANTS

To understand God's master plan, you must understand the covenants He made with man.

Noahic Covenant

The Lord saw that the wickedness of man was great, and He saw that every intent and thoughts of man's heart was continually evil. God saw the wickedness in the world and knew that He needed to raise up the Redeemer. Therefore, He chose to shepherd a flock from which the Savior could come. At one point, the world was so vile that God took a drastic measure. His first attempt to set aside a chosen people after the fall of man comes in the story of the Flood.

Noah found favor in God. He was counted as a righteous man, blameless among the people of his time, and he walked with God. God decided to wipe the slate clean and start over with Noah. He sent a flood to destroy every living creature with the exception of Noah, his immediate family, and some animals. The flood was a sort of reset button returning the world to a time resembling the second day of creation when the waters covered the earth.

Noah did all the Lord commanded him to do. He built an ark for his family and animals. For forty days the flood continued, and as the waters increased they lifted the ark high and covered the mountains to a depth of more than twenty feet. Every living thing that moved on the earth perished. Only Noah and those with him on the ark survived.

The waters flooded the earth for a hundred and fifty days. When God finally called Noah out of the ark and onto dry ground, the first thing Noah did was build an altar to the Lord and offer burnt sacrifices on it. As a side note, isn't this what we should also do when we emerge from a storm in our lives, offer up our sacrifice of praise?

God accepted the offering and blessed Noah and his family. So God blessed Noah and his sons and said to them: "Be fruitful and multiply, and fill the earth."14

After the Flood, God made a covenant with Noah: "Thus I establish My covenant with you: Never again shall all flesh be cut off by the waters of the flood; never again shall there be a flood to destroy the earth. I set My rainbow in the cloud, and it shall be for the sign of the covenant between Me and the earth."15

Interestingly, there is a rainbow encircling the throne of God. It is as if God gave us a piece of Heaven as a sign of His promise. Every time we see a rainbow in the sky, we are reminded of the Noahic covenant God made more than four thousand years ago. Throughout the centuries, His pledge has never been broken. This demonstration of God's faithfulness to man is a testimony of His love for us.

Abrahamic Covenant

After the Flood, which was designed to clean the world and to propagate a bloodline for the Redeemer, the people once again became victims of their own sin and a corrupt people who threatened the coming of the Redeemer.

Because God had promised to never destroy the world again, He took a different approach to the situation. He knew the plan and costs of His divine goal, so this time He chose to set aside a group of people to be called His own.

He called Abraham to be the father of His chosen people, the Jews. Basically, God selected a population from which the Redeemer would arise. He selected a nation to breed the coming Messiah who would save the *entire* world.

God called Abraham out of Mesopotamia and promised to give his offspring the land of Canaan (the land that today includes modern Israel, all the land of the Palestinians [the West Bank and Gaza], some of Egypt and Syria, all of Jordan, and some of Saudi Arabia and Iraq). He also promised that Abraham's descendants would be as numerous as the stars. God said, "Leave your country, your people and your father's household and go to the land I will show you. I will make you into a great nation and I will bless you; I will make your name great, and you will be a blessing."16

It is important to understand that the Jewish people were chosen to be a vehicle and a herald for God's plan. The Bible goes on to say that all peoples on earth will be blessed through them. What an awesome responsibility and privilege!!! However, it is mistakenly perceived that the Jewish people are the chosen people because they will be the only ones to live with God. This is not true. The

Redeemer was to be for everyone. Furthermore, careful consideration about Jewish beginnings will shed light on this controversy. Ask yourself this: Abraham was the first Jew, but what was he before that? He was a Gentile!

God's covenant with Abraham and his descendants involved two interactions. Both were blood exchanges: one of animal blood (a shadow of things that were) and the other of human blood (a shadow of things that were to come).

The Lord told Abraham to bring Him a heifer, a goat, and a ram (each three-years-old) along with a dove and a young pigeon. Abraham brought all these to God, cut them in two, and arranged the halves opposite each other (except for the birds, which he did not cut in half).

In ancient custom, people would make a covenant by walking between the halves of a sacrificed animal as part of their oaths. (The book of Jeremiah demonstrates this ancient custom too.) They would walk through the blood, arm in arm, down the middle of the sacrificed animals. In essence, they were saying if I break this covenant, this is what you may do to me.

Abraham did not get a chance to walk the blood path with God. Instead, God placed Abraham into a deep sleep, and then He appeared and passed between the pieces alone. This signified that God assumed the full responsibility of the covenant. Therefore, all Abraham and mankind could do was to have faith and live out God's promises.

Then the Lord returned to renew and expand the blood covenant. God promised Abraham and his descendants that:

*Abraham would be the father of many nations.

*They would be very fruitful.

*The covenant would be an everlasting one.

*He would be their God.

*The whole land of Canaan would be an everlasting possession.

This time, though, Abraham had a responsibility in the cutting of the covenant. God said to Abraham, "As for you, you must keep My covenant, you and your descendants after you for the generations to come."17

Circumcision was deemed the sign of the covenant. This act of circumcision, cutting the foreskin of the penis, was to stand as a continual reminder that God had cut a covenant with Abraham and his descendants. It was a way for Abraham to pass the covenant and blessings down through the generations. The Israelites were to circumcise every eight-day-old male among them. Abraham himself, as well as his family, servants, and livestock, had to come under the covenant.

God said that this covenant in the flesh was to be an everlasting covenant. Any uncircumcised male, who had not been circumcised in the flesh, was to be cut off from his people because he had broken God's covenant.

God's instructions were clear, His rules were rigid, and the consequences of disobedience were grim. There was too much at stake, and God had to make sure that His chosen people would make the way for the Redeemer.

Beyr Reyes

Mosiac Covenant

According to the Abrahamic Covenant, God chose the Jewish people to be separate from the rest of the world. They were to live as a distinct nation who worshiped the Lord as their only god. His plan was to create a group of people from which the Savior would arise.

However, once again, sin ensnared men, even God's chosen group. The Jewish people had blended into the world and were no longer a separate nation. They had relinquished their territorial rights to Canaan and were residing among the other nations like Egypt. Furthermore, they had taken up pagan practices and worship of idols and pagan gods.

Ultimately, the Jews were not living up to the promises in the Abrahamic covenant. They had forfeited their right to the land, had become subject of other nations instead of rising above them, and most importantly, they were not faithful to their one true God.

God, once again, had to set the Jewish people apart in order to carry out His plan to save the world. God called Moses to fulfill the job this time. Moses led the people in a mass exodus out of Egypt.

Shortly after wandering in the desert, Moses was called to Mount Sinai by God. Here, God wrote the book of Genesis Himself and gave Moses the Law (the book of the covenant) by which the Jewish people were to live. The tablets of the Testimony were inscribed on both sides, front and back.

Moses left the mountain carrying the two stones containing the Ten Commandments. In those times, just like today, it was customary for each involved party to receive a copy of a contract. However, God intended for His people to have both copies (both tablets). He didn't need a reminder or any proof of His intentions because He never intended to renege on His word.

When Moses reached the Israelite camp, he found the people worshiping a golden calf instead of the Lord. In anger, he threw the tablets to the ground, breaking them to pieces at the foot of the mountain. Needless to say, Moses had to return to the mountain to obtain a new set of tablets.

When Moses returned again to the Israelites, he read the book of the covenant, and the people agreed to obey the law. This covenant, like the previous ones, was put into effect with blood. An animal was cut, and the people came under the covenant by being sprinkled with its blood. Moses did this while saying, "This is the blood of the covenant that the Lord has made with you in accordance with all these words."18

Although people are inclined to believe that God gave the law as written only on tablets, actually God said, "I will put my law in their minds and write it on their hearts."19 He did not write the law only on tablets, but also on our hearts and lives.

We know the law is from God because He created us and wrote the law on our hearts. Even someone who has never heard the Ten Commandments still knows them; they just call it a different name—morality. That inner sense of morality is nothing more than God's stamp on our hearts.

So what was the purpose of the Mosiac Covenant of law? The purpose of the law was two-fold: to keep the Jewish people set apart from all others and to reveal the need for the Savior.

The Jewish people knew that they were to live separately, both physically and spiritually, from the rest of the world. This was the basis of the Abrahamic Covenant. However, they were not given any details of how to carry out this lifestyle. Furthermore, they were given no consequences (except for being cut off from God, which should have been good enough) for their disobedience.

According to the Bible, all Scripture is God-breathed and is useful for teaching, rebuking, correcting, and training in righteousness. God instituted the Law to give the Jewish people guidelines and rules to make their path straight and less ambiguous. When they broke the law, the punishment was severe and often led to the death of the individual, as well as the entire family. The law and consequences may be seen as too harsh on occasions; however, the severity was required to set apart the people and make the way for the Savior.

The Mosiac Covenant and the dispensation of the law was more than a set or rules and instructions, or morality. In light of the law, sin was revealed and specifically defined. The strength of sin is the law. The law was stringent and showed the Jewish people that there was (and is) no way that good deeds and behavior would ever be enough. It was (and is) impossible to meet all the commands, even on a given day. The sting of death is sin, and the law revealed our need for a savior. It became evident that there could be no other way to fulfill the law.

Davidic Covenant

When the Lord rejected Saul as king over Israel, He called the prophet Samuel to anoint one of Jesse's sons as the next king. When David, the youngest of his sons, was presented to Samuel, the Lord told Samuel that he was the one and to rise and anoint him. So Samuel took the oil and anointed David. From that day on, the Spirit of the Lord was upon David in power.

Later, God instructed Nathan (David's prophet) to give David a message from Him. He said that He would make David's name great, provide a place for His people Israel, and give David rest from all his enemies. God said that after David's death, He would raise up his offspring to succeed him and would establish the throne of his kingdom forever. The Lord said that He would be his father, and he would be His son.

Although there is no covenant sign mentioned in the Davidic covenant, the most reasonable symbol of it would be the throne or ruling. The Messiah is the root and the offspring of David. He will rule over the nations with an iron scepter and carry the title KING OF KINGS AND LORD OF LORDS.

Chapter 5
NEW COVENANT

Something was seriously wrong with the Israelite covenant. Not on God's side, but on that of the Jewish people. The fault was with the people. They did not have the heart to obey the commandments, and God knew it. Unlike Abraham, they did not believe and were not faithful.

God promised a new covenant prophesied through His prophet Jeremiah.[20]

> *"Behold, the days are coming," says the Lord, "When I will make a new covenant with the house of Israel and with the house of Judah—not according to the covenant that I made with their fathers in the day that I took them by the hand to lead them out of the land of Egypt, My covenant which they broke, though I was a husband to them," says the Lord. "But this is the covenant that I will make with the house of Israel after those days," says the Lord. "I will put My law in their minds, and write it on their hearts; and I will be their God, and they shall be My people. No more shall every man teach his neighbor, and every man his brother, saying, 'Know the Lord,' for they all shall know Me, from the least of them to the greatest of them," says the Lord. "For I will forgive their iniquity, and their sin I will remember no more." (Jer. 31:31-34 NKJV)*

This is what God the Lord says:

> "I, the Lord, have called you in righteousness; I will take hold of your hand. I will keep you and will make you to be a covenant for the people and a light for the Gentiles, to open eyes that are blind, to free captives from prison and to release from the dungeon those who sit in darkness. See, the former things have taken place, and new things I declare; before they spring into being I announce them to you." (Is. 42:6-9 NIV)

This new covenant involved redemption, which was something the Jewish people were already familiar with and practiced regularly with the animal sacrifices. The new covenant promised a coming Messiah who would redeem the people. The Lord told Joshua that He would bring His servant, the Branch, and remove the sin of this land in a single day.

The Prophesied Messiah

God used His prophets to reveal His master plan and foretell the coming of the Messiah who would fulfill this new covenant. The prophet Isaiah provided the most detailed description of Him:

> Here is my servant, whom I uphold, my chosen one in whom I delight; I will put my Spirit on him and he will bring justice to the nations. He will not shout or cry out, or raise his voice in the streets. A bruised reed he will not break, and a smoldering wick he will not snuff out. In faithfulness he will bring forth justice; he will not falter or be discouraged till he establishes justice on earth. In his law the islands will put their hope. (Is. 42:1-4 NIV)

> He was despised and rejected by men, a man of sorrows, and familiar with suffering. Like one from whom men hide their faces he was despised, and we esteemed him not. Surely he took up our

infirmities and carried our sorrows, yet we considered him stricken by God, smitten by him, and afflicted. (Is. 53:3-4 NIV)

But he was pierced for our transgressions, he was crushed for our iniquities; the punishment that brought us peace was upon him, and by his wounds we are healed. (Is. 53:5 NIV) *They will look on me, the one they have pierced, and they will mourn for him as one mourns for an only child, and grieve bitterly for him as one grieves for a firstborn son.* (Zech 12:10 NIV)

We all, like sheep, have gone astray, each of us has turned to his own way; and the Lord has laid on him the iniquity of us all. He was oppressed and afflicted, yet he did not open his mouth; he was led like a lamb to the slaughter, and as a sheep before her shearers is silent, so he did not open his mouth. (Is. 53:6-7 NIV)

He was assigned a grave with the wicked, and with the rich in his death, though he had done no violence, nor was any deceit in his mouth. Yet it was the Lord's will to crush him and cause him to suffer, and though the Lord makes his life a guilt offering, he will see his offspring and prolong his days, and the will of the Lord will prosper in his hand. After the suffering of his soul, he will see the light of life and be satisfied; by his knowledge my righteous servant will justify many, and he will bear their iniquities. Therefore I will give him a portion among the great, and he will divide the spoils with the strong, because he poured out his life unto death, and was numbered with the transgressors. For he bore the sin of many, and made intercession for the transgressors. (Is. 53:9-12 NIV)

The Jewish people were given signs of the coming of the Messiah. Religious festivals, New Moon celebrations, and

Sabbath days, these were shadows of the things that were to come. The people had been rehearsing for the coming of our Savior for many years. Nevertheless, many of them missed the Messiah because of their blindness.

God blinded the minds of unbelievers so that they could not see the light of the gospel of the glory of Christ. He blinded their eyes and deadened their hearts, so they could neither see nor understand. The Jewish people had to be blind or they would have never allowed the death of King Jesus.

Jesus the Redeemer

The thief comes to steal, kill, and destroy, but Jesus came to give everlasting life. Death has a right to mankind and every man shall die for his own sin. However, Jesus became us on the cross. He was the ultimate Passover lamb whose blood prevents death. All sin was placed on Him for atonement. He bore it and died in our place; He paid our debt of sin. Unlike all the animal sacrifices, though, this sacrifice will last for eternity.

The Redeemer had to be fully man and fully God at the same time, because he had to be able to die, yet still be able to conquer death. If the Redeemer were only flesh, he could not have conquered death and would have been subject to sin and death under the law. Had the Redeemer not been flesh, He could have never died and thus fulfilled the redemption price. *Jesus was God in the flesh.* God came to earth and lived and died as a man. He took our place.

Not only did the Redeemer satisfy the price of sin, He conquered death. After death on the cross, Jesus entered the Most High Place and made the ultimate atonement for us. He ripped the curtain that separated us from God.

Then, He entered the belly of the earth, into the fiery pits of Hell, where He took the keys to death. The Bible says that He who descended is the very one who ascended higher than all the heavens in order to fill the entire universe.

It is interesting to note that God tends to only go to places where He is invited. He doesn't barge into our lives, but allows us the freewill to decide whether we want a relationship with Him or not. At any time, God could have taken the keys to death. He is that powerful, you know. Yet, He devised a beautiful plan in which death and Hell gladly accepted and rejoiced over the death of Jesus; they openly welcomed Him in. Little did they know, though, who was about to enter!

If we accept Jesus as our savior and redeemer then He takes our place in death. To accept Jesus and be saved from sin and death, you must confess with your mouth, "Jesus is Lord," and believe in your heart that God raised Him from the dead. For it is with your heart that you believe and are justified, and it is with your mouth that you confess and are saved.

New Creature in Christ

You were taught, with regard to your former way of life, to put off your old self, which is being corrupted by its deceitful desires; to be made new in the attitude of your minds; and to put on the new self, created to be like God in true righteousness and holiness. (Eph 4:22-24 NIV)

We are to put on the new self, which is being renewed in knowledge in the image of its Creator. Through the death and resurrection of Jesus Christ, we will have a new glorious body, because flesh and blood cannot inherit the kingdom of God. Our mortal bodies must become immortal. When we are in Christ, we have a new mind, a mind of Christ. We are no longer to conform to the pattern of this world; we are to be transformed by the renewing of our mind.

God gives us a body as He has determined, and so will it be with the resurrection of the dead. A natural body is sown, but a spiritual body is raised. The body that is sown is perishable, it is raised imperishable; that which is sown in dishonor and weakness is raised in glory and power. Just as we have the likeness of the earthly man, we will also bear the likeness of the man from heaven. In a flash, in the twinkling of an eye, we will be changed.

Jesus gave us a glimpse of what this glorified body looks like when He was transfigured on the mountain. His clothes became dazzling white, whiter than they could be bleached by anyone in the world, as bright as a flash of lightning. The appearance of His face changed and it shone like the sun.

Jesus provided healing (both spiritually and physically) for our body and mind. Until Adam and Eve ate from the Tree of Knowledge, they never knew about sickness or death. However, when they came to know of these things, they became susceptible and subject to them. When Jesus died, He took our infirmities to the cross with Him. By His stripes we are healed. All illnesses and disease were crucified with Him, and man gained the power to overcome them.

Holy Spirit

God promised to give you a new heart and put a new spirit in you; He will remove from you your heart of stone and give you a heart of flesh. Jesus said He would send what the Father has promised. God sent the Holy Spirit.

Jesus received the Holy Spirit when He was baptized. As soon as He came up out of the water, Heaven was opened, and the Spirit of God (the Holy Spirit) descended on Him as a dove. A voice came from Heaven: "You are my Son, whom I love; with you I am well pleased." John the Baptist gave this testimony: "I saw the Spirit come down from Heaven as a dove and remain on him. I would not have known him, except that the one who sent me to baptize with water told me, 'The man on whom you see the Spirit come down and remain is He who will baptize with the Holy Spirit.' I have seen and I testify that this is the Son of God."21

When Jesus commissioned the disciples after His resurrection, He breathed on them, and said to them, "Receive the Holy Spirit."22 "Behold, I send the Promise of My Father upon you; but wait in the city of Jerusalem until you are endued with power from on high."23 On the day of Pentecost all the disciples were together. Suddenly a sound from Heaven like a rushing, mighty wind filled the entire house. They saw what seemed to be tongues of fire that separated and came to rest, one upon each of them. Everyone was filled with the Holy Spirit and began to speak in other tongues as the Spirit enabled them.

The Holy Spirit is many things to us. First and foremost, it is the Spirit of God dwelling with us. No longer will God live in a temple and be separated from man with a curtain. Instead, He sent His Holy Spirit to inhabit in the temple of our living bodies. The Holy Spirit marks us and seals us for the day of redemption.

Jesus said that the Counselor, the Holy Spirit, whom the Father will send in His name, will teach you all things. He will guide you into all truth. Jesus is our advocate on high, speaking to the Father in our defense. The Holy Spirit will speak what He hears, and will tell you what is yet to come. He is the Comforter from the Father; He will abide with you forever.

When Jesus died for us, He carried the punishment for our transgressions and iniquities. Once the stain of sin was removed from man, he was restored to his original power and authority. The only difference was that instead of being caretaker of the garden, man inherited the earth. Furthermore, we are no longer subject to Satan's rule if we are new creatures in Christ. Jesus said, "The prince of this world will be driven out."[24] We are given a new anointing with power and authority through the Holy Spirit. In the name of Jesus, we are given the power to cast out demons and lay hands on the sick, so that they shall recover.

The Holy Spirit enables gifts in our lives. Although there are different kinds of gifts, all are from the same Spirit. These gifts are for the purpose of building up the Church and include wisdom and knowledge, faith, healing, miraculous powers, prophecy, discernment, and speaking in and interpretation of tongues. Are all people prophets? Do all work miracles? Do all have gifts of healing? Do all speak in tongues? God grants the gifts of the Holy Spirit as He determines; however, we are to eagerly desire (but not covet) all these gifts.

Joel prophesied the Holy Spirit. God said that He would pour out His Spirit on all flesh; our sons and daughters would prophesy, old men would dream dreams, and young men would see visions. If you have received Christ as your

Redeemer and Lord, but have not yet received the Holy Spirit, all you have to do is ask for it. On the last and greatest day of the Feast of Tabernacles (the day of the water-drawing ceremony), Jesus stood and said in a loud voice, "If anyone is thirsty, let him come to me and drink."[25] Jesus told a Samaritan woman that He gives living water to those who ask. Are you thirsty for the refreshing water of the Holy Spirit?

Beyr Reyes

Chapter 6
SATAN'S PLAN

Before we can discuss Satan's plan, we first must answer the question: *Who is Satan?*

Before he became Satan, Satan was Lucifer. Lucifer was an archangel in Heaven. He was a model of perfection, full of wisdom, and perfect in beauty. Every precious stone with settings and mountings of gold adorned him. The word Lucifer means morning star; he was the bright and shining one.

Lucifer was created and anointed as a guardian cherub ordained by God. His job was to lead worship and to set the atmosphere in Heaven. Clearly, he had the power and wisdom right from the start to engage beings and draw them in. After all, he was anointed by God for this skill.

Lucifer was blameless in his ways from the day he was created until wickedness was found in him. The word wicked literally means lawless. His heart became proud on account of his beauty and splendor, and it corrupted his wisdom. Pride led him to think that he could rise higher than God Himself. In his heart he said that he would ascend to Heaven, raise his throne above God, sit enthroned on the mount—on the utmost heights of the sacred mountain—and make himself like the Most High. Lucifer transformed into the evil dragon.

A war broke out in Heaven. Michael and his angels fought against the dragon (Lucifer) and his angels. But Lucifer was not strong enough, and he and his angels lost their place in Heaven. This ancient serpent called the devil, the one who leads the whole world astray, was hurled to the earth, his angels with him.

Satan was given dominion over earth as attested by his titles, prince of this world and god of this world. Since then, he constantly accuses creation before the throne of God day and night. He despises man because man was created to be higher than him, and it is his opinion that he should be the highest being, higher even than God. In addition, perhaps he is jealous of the relationship of God and man and wonders how God could love man more than him, or how God could think any being more beautiful than him. Until the creation of Adam and Eve, Lucifer was the most beautiful creation of God. However, Eve was the grand finale of God's creation. It's no wonder Satan approached and sought to sully Eve first.

Separate Man From God

Regardless of his motives, Satan immediately set out on his initial plan—to separate man from God. He sought to corrupt man and to smite God. He knew that in a corrupted state, man could no longer dwell with God and would be expelled from His presence like he, himself, was.

Satan was in the Garden when God laid down the rule for Adam and Eve. He played upon that rule and twisted it. He sought to instill in man the desire to be a god too. This desire was something he could identify with, and it seems likely that he would think others would feel the same way if presented with the idea.

Satan told Adam and Eve that they would be like God, having knowledge of all good and evil, if they ate the fruit of the forbidden tree. Note that this is common trickery that he still uses today. However, be self-controlled and alert. Your enemy the devil prowls around like a roaring lion looking for someone to devour. He lies in wait to catch the helpless and drag them off. Adam and Eve were his first victims.

After the incident in the Garden, Satan continued to try to separate man from God. (Notice that he doesn't try to separate God from man.) Eventually, due to his continual sowing of corruption and his success in leading people astray, creation had become so vile that God flooded the world in order to start all over.

Destroy Abrahamic Covenant

Satan knew that God was up to something when God struck the covenant with Abraham. He eavesdropped on God's promise to Abraham and learned that a messiah, God's blessing to the earth, would be a descendent of Abraham through his son Isaac. Satan, at that point, had to develop a new plan with new targets, namely this new nation of people.

Ever since, the Jewish people have been persecuted and constantly attacked. Satan desired the annihilation of them so that the Messiah could not come. He immediately sought to destroy the people, thus birthing the idea of genocide.

At one point, Satan had the Israelites under his thumb. They were trapped by thick oppression in Egypt. Despite this, the more they were subjugated, the more they multiplied and spread, so much so that the Egyptians came to dread the Israelites. Then, the king of Egypt ordered the Jewish midwives to kill all the male newborn babies. If all the male infants were slain, the Jewish race would disappear within a single generation. But many midwives feared God and His judgment more than the king, and did not do as the king commanded them. One child, Moses, narrowly escaped this genocide. God chose him to lead His people out of Egypt.

Later, the Lord instructed Moses and Joshua to completely blot out the memory of Amalek (the Israelite's enemy nation) from under heaven. However, the Israelites failed to do so. When Saul (the first king of Israel) battled the Amalekites, he destroyed all the people but took King Agag alive. Many years later, Hamen the Agagite (an Agagite is considered either a literal descendant of Agag or an anti-Semite) played a key role in another of Satan's genocide attempts as recorded in the Book of Esther. Letters were sent into all the king's lands to destroy, kill, and annihilate all the Jewish people in one day, the thirteenth day of the twelfth month. Once again, though, Satan's plan was thwarted, this time through the faith and obedience of one young Jewish girl, Esther, who God raised to the position of Royal Queen for such a time as this.

Prevent the Messiah's Coming

Satan knew from God's conversation with Abraham that Jesus was coming. In actuality, this was something he had already heard in the Garden. God told the serpent that He would put enmity between him and the woman, and between his offspring and hers. Her offspring would crush the serpent's head, and Satan would in turn strike His heel. Eve heard this conversation too and knew that her offspring would restore order. Perhaps she thought her first born, Cain, would be this savior. Hypothetically, what if Cain grew up hearing his mother tell the story and thinking that he had this great task at hand? His stress and frustration of not completing this task may have led him to begrudgingly offer a sacrifice to God and to kill Abel out of jealousy. Or, what if Satan saw that Abel was favored by God and would likely be the line of the offspring responsible for his demise? What if Satan incited Cain to kill Abel? Both scenarios are just considerations, but interesting ones nonetheless.

Satan knew that the Messiah was coming; he just didn't know when. He closely watched the prophets over many years and assembled the key prophecies. He knew the time was drawing near when he began to see the prophetic signs. When Jesus was born, the Eastern Star heralded His birth. Satan saw this and moved Herod to slay all the male infants. Although this plan failed, Satan later witnessed the death of Jesus.

It seems certain that when Satan witnessed the crucifixion of Jesus he was drunk with the happiness of thinking he was victorious. Imagine his surprise when Jesus showed up in Hell to take the keys of death away from him. Without a doubt, he was glad to see Jesus leave when He ascended to Heaven. However, at Pentecost when the Holy Spirit was poured out on all mankind, instead of seeing one Jesus, Satan saw thousands of men with the Holy Spirit in them. Essentially, what Satan saw were thousands of versions of Jesus. Satan thought that he could win by killing Jesus, but he didn't understand God's master plan or he would have never sought Jesus' death.

Many unbelievers wonder why Jesus returned to Heaven after the resurrection instead of staying on earth and ruling the nations, as it had been prophesied. Perhaps you've wondered this too. Jesus left for two reasons. First, as the bridegroom, He went away to prepare a place for us. Secondly, in the end, all of earth will be destroyed. Had He not delayed His reign and rule, we would have never been born, never received Him, and never become His own. He doesn't want anyone to perish; He wants *all* to come to repentance.

Counterfeit Christianity and the Bible

Once Satan realized who and what Jesus was, he had to devise a new plan. Enraged, he went off to make war against the rest of the offspring—those who obey God's commandments and hold to the testimony of Jesus. He seeks to counterfeit religion, the Bible, the Church, and Jesus.

God put a strong desire in every person's heart to worship Him. However, under Satan's influence, man has perverted this desire. Instead, man seeks fame, wealth, and control of people and society. Satan understands this necessity to worship (after all, he was created to lead it in Heaven). In the end, he will come as an "angel of light," claim to be God, and demand to be worshiped by every person on earth. This is what he has always wanted and has waited thousands of years to receive. The whole world will worship Satan, thinking they are worshiping God.

So how could the entire earth go from worshiping God to worshiping Satan? It seems too farfetched to be feasible. Yet, we know that in the end times of the world people will worship the beast and take his mark. What could possibly be the driving force for such an extreme revolution?

Satan is distracting people from the true gospel by weaving a little information from the Bible with a lot of false doctrines. By convincing others that spirituality is foolish, he seeks to destroy the spiritual part in man by persuading the natural part that it can get along without the spiritual one.26 Once man loses his spiritual aspect, he does not receive the things of the Spirit of God, for they are foolishness to him; he cannot understand them because they are spiritually discerned.

Satan also targets Christians. If you are in Christ, you are supposed to be a new creature. If you continue in your old ways then it begs the question: Are you truly in Christ? Christ is the source of eternal salvation for all *who obey him*. The verse does not stop at the word *all*; it provides a condition. Furthermore, the old adage *once saved always saved* is a lie from the devil. God does not walk away from us, but we can walk away from God. Jesus said that He gives eternal life and that we shall never perish; no man can pluck us out of His hand. To pluck means to be carried off by force, like the action of a thief. Neither Satan nor any outside force can steal you from the Lord as long as you meet the conditions.

The *once saved always saved* adage is a false doctrine because it clearly contradicts the scriptures in nearly every book of the Bible. Despite this, it is a popular doctrine because it allows people to believe that once you accept Jesus as your savior it is impossible for you to sin, fall from grace, and be eternally lost. It deceives many into thinking that they will still reap eternal life, even if they give in to the flesh. People feel safe even though they don't examine their lives, study the Bible, or repent of sin. The Bible is very clear in that your name *can* be blotted out of the Book of Life. The Lord told Moses that He will blot out of His book whoever has sinned against Him.

We must avoid falling away from God, and we must bear fruit or be cast off. The Bible says that if anyone does not remain in Christ, he is like a branch that is thrown away and withers; such branches are picked up, thrown into the fire, and burned. For those who were once saved yet fall away, a great punishment awaits. Anyone (including a child of God) who has denied the faith is worse than a nonbeliever. If they have escaped the corruption of the world by knowing Jesus Christ and are entangled again, they are worse off in the end than they were at the beginning.

> *It is impossible for those who have once been enlightened, who have tasted the heavenly gift, who have shared in the Holy Spirit, who have tasted the goodness of the word of God and the powers of the coming age, if they fall away, to be brought back to repentance, because to their loss they are crucifying the Son of God all over again and subjecting him to public disgrace. Land that drinks in the rain often falling on it and that produces a crop useful to those for whom it is farmed receives the blessing of God. But land that produces thorns and thistles is worthless and is in danger of being cursed. In the end it will be burned.* (Heb 6:4-8 NIV)

Satan has divided the Church into denominations to serve as further distractions. People get so lost in debating the Bible that they forget to live by its words. At the same time, Satan is trying to bring everyone under a one world religion so that he may rule. He already has his own synagogues and churches, and some even have the words

Jesus or Christ as part of the name of their denomination. The Bible states that there will be those who say they are Jews and are not, but are a synagogue of Satan. This bait and switch is yet another way to deceive people and draw them over to Satan's side.

Part of the reason Satan will be successful in instituting his false religion is because people will have itching ears, and he will scratch them. People will no longer hold to sound doctrine. They won't want to hear how they could go to Hell, or anything to do with maintaining holiness. Instead, to suit their own desires, they will gather around teachers who say what their itching ears want to hear. They will be more interested in how to achieve prosperity than how to attain eternal life.

New Age religions, which are based on self-centered beliefs instead of God-centered ones, are ushering in the false religion of Satan. They are designed to get in touch with the inner man. Essentially, Satan is going back to original plan in the Garden by making man think that he could be a god and that he does not need the Lord.

Although New Age religions concentrate on becoming gods, people are actually robbed of their power and authority instead of being given it. Christians fall prey to this thief as well. Jesus said that all power is given unto Him in Heaven and in earth. If you are a new creature in Christ, you will have this power; if you aren't, then you won't.

Satan has also sought to instill narrow-mindedness in Christians. For example, he has some folks believing that the King James Version of the Bible is the only true Bible. They struggle to understand the archaic language in this version and eventually give up trying to read the Bible. The devil successfully keeps God's children ignorant of the Word by using this trick.

When it comes to pitting one Bible version against another, the most important thing to remember is to use caution when reading only one version of the Bible. It is important to read several different versions of a passage to absorb the complete meaning. Saturate yourself with the Word. If you're used to reading only one version, try reading different versions in parallel to gain insight and open new perspectives. In addition, be sure to exercise caution when choosing Bible versions, as some have slightly altered language to water down the text and make it more seeker-friendly, instead of telling it like it is. Beware of bibles that are paraphrased; while these are good to get an overall description of the text, use a direct translation of the Bible to attain the truth.

The Bible is a living document that speaks to us individually. In reality, there are thousands of interpretations. However, in addition to *interpretations* are counterfeit *translations* of the Bible. Such translations very subtly distort God's word. For example, some translations replace the word "virgin" in the Old Testament with "young woman," thus raising questions as to the virgin birth of Jesus Christ. Other translations that are gender-neutral blur the lines between gender and sexuality and open the door to tolerance of homosexuality, which is something that the Bible clearly indicates is wrong.

Be on the watch for New Age translations of the Bible. New Age doctrines are infiltrating the church today. Many times, when New Agers say "the Christ," they mean "the Christ within." They are not referring to Jesus of Nazareth, but are referring to their concept of the Christ, or

THE BIG PICTURE

essentially an illumination of their inner self. It is important for Christians to use great discernment. In the end times of the world, many Christians will lose sight of the difference. They will be confused by the New Age rhetoric, which twists the Biblical truth of being filled with the Holy Spirit. Some New Agers believe and teach that there is a god in everyone—not *The God*, but a god.

We have been warned about altering the Bible. This isn't referring to different translations, but to the changing of the original text, the sources in the original languages used to create the translated Bible versions into other languages. Some New Age books include many of the stories in the Old and New Testaments. However, don't be deceived; they contain a little bit of truth mixed in with a whole lot of lies. The old bait-and-switch game again. Don't fall for the devil's tricks. The New Age leaders are using this same technique of exploiting Bible snippets to bring legitimacy to their beliefs and doctrines. Nearly everyone believes the fundamentals of the Bible, and New Age leaders are banking on it. By using Bible text they can put the reader on a path—a path that they use to quickly redirect and send the traveler in the wrong direction—<u>away</u> from the one true God.

The Bible is a living document through which our great Lord speaks. The goal should be to read it every day. If you find the King James Version confusing or hard to read, don't let that keep you from getting into the Word. Try a different version. A quick internet-based review of Bible versions will reveal that most Bible scholars agree that the best versions of the Bible in no particular order include the *King James Version*, the *New International Version*, the *New King James Version*, and the *American Standard Bible*.

Counterfeit Jesus

Satan knows that Jesus is coming again, thus his days are numbered. At this point, he is just trying to buy time before the second coming of Christ and take with him to Hell as many souls as he can. The more people he keeps from accepting Christ as their Savior, the more God's heart will mourn over His lost children, and the more company Satan will have in Hell. (Undoubtedly, he is looking for souls to rule over.)

Jesus said that we will not see Him again until the Jewish people say, "Blessed is He who comes in the name of the Lord."27 Therefore, Satan wants to keep the Jewish people from knowing their messiah because this will initiate the second coming. Because they are still looking for their Messiah, they are a target for Satan's plan. Instead of calling on Jesus, Satan wants then to call on another name so that Jesus won't come. As a result, Satan sends many false messiahs.

Jesus foretold the coming of false messiahs and stated, "Take heed that no one deceives you. For many will come in My name, saying, 'I am the Christ (Messiah),' and will deceive many."28 The Bible provides a warning for folks who accept those who preach another Jesus, receive a different spirit, or entertain a different gospel. It tells us that there will be false apostles and deceitful workers who transform themselves into apostles of Christ. Satan himself can transform into an angel of light; therefore, it is no surprise that his ministers can also transform themselves into ministers who appear to be righteous.

In the end times, Satan will go so far as to counterfeit the Holy Trinity. While he will attempt to masquerade as the Father, he will raise the antichrist to be an imitation

Jesus and a false prophet to forge the Holy Spirit. The antichrist will ascend from the pit in an attempt to imitate the resurrection of Lord Jesus Christ. Satan will put his spirit into man like God did with Jesus, and thus create the antichrist. In appearance, the antichrist will have two horns like a lamb. Of course, Jesus Christ is referred to as the "Lamb of God" or the "Lamb which takes away the sins of the world"; therefore, a lamb symbolizes Jesus Christ, the Savior of the world. The antichrist will appear as a counterfeit lamb, and those who claim to be Christians, yet lack discernment, will accept him. He will exercise his authority on earth for forty-two months during the end times. (This is synonymous with the three-and-a-half-year ministry of Jesus on earth.) The antichrist (the lawless one) will work according to the edicts of Satan, with all power, signs, and lying wonders. The false prophet will perform miraculous deeds on his behalf. With these performances he will delude those who receive the mark of the beast. Sadly, many will be deceived and will be cast into eternal darkness, where there will be wailing and gnashing of teeth.

The antichrist (Satan incarnate) will blaspheme God, but people will be deceived and not see through it. They will continue to worship him in his false religion. On the contrary, when Jesus (God incarnate) sought to lift up the name of God, the people were deceived then too, especially the Pharisees. They did not see Him for who He was. Yet, in a strange twist, Jesus was accused of blaspheme and was crucified for it (blasphemers are put to death), while Satan will be worshiped despite it.

Have you fallen prey to Satan's trickery? Do you think that the Bible is just a book of old stories? Do you think that the Church has replaced Israel? Do you think that

Jesus didn't exist, or was just another prophet? Do you think that the gifts of the spirit and the power conferred by the name of Jesus died with the apostles? Do you believe that once you are saved, you are always saved?

Chapter 7
IN THE END

At the end of days, when the times reach their fulfillment, all things in Heaven and on earth will be brought together. But before this happens, the Lord will be sure to give plenty of warning to the obstinate and rebellious people.

> *Woe to the obstinate children, to those who carry out plans that are not mine, forming an alliance, but not by my Spirit, heaping sin upon sin.* (Is. 30:1 NIV) *In repentance and rest is your salvation, in quietness and trust is your strength, <u>but you would have none of it.</u>* (Is. 30:15 NIV [emphasis added])

Nevertheless, as Peter described in the Bible, in the last days scoffers will come and follow their own evil desires. They will say, "Where is this 'coming' he promised? Ever since our fathers died, everything goes on as it has since the beginning of creation." Sound familiar??

Just remember, one of God's days is equal to a thousand of our years. If you divide a thousand years (a day to God) by twenty-four, you get the amount of years equal to one of God's hours–approximately forty years. John tells us that the antichrist comes in the last hour and that is how we know the end is near. Chances are, with all the signs of the end times, we are somewhere in that forty years now. What time is it on *your* watch?

Signs of the End of Times

Despite all the warnings, folks are still reluctant to accept their free gift of salvation and walk in the promises, even in the face of imminent signs. These signs can be seen everywhere we look in society, and many prophecies have been fulfilled in the past one hundred years.

World, social, and natural events are heralding the end time. Nations are rising against other nations and kingdoms against other kingdoms; there are famines and earthquakes all over the earth. All these proceedings are the beginning of birth pains. If you doubt any of this, just read the list below. This by no means is a comprehensive list; however, it will easily reveal the state of impending times. Many books are dedicated to this topic.

* *The nation of Israel will be born in a day.* The world witnessed the rebirth of the state of Israel on May 14, 1948. In the history of the world, no people or country has ever gone out of existence for as long as 2,000 years and then been reborn. It was a miracle recorded in the history books.

* *The Jewish people will return to their ancient homeland.* Recently, there has been a massive immigration of Jewish people from the US, Europe, and the Soviet Republic. The people have returned first from the east then from the west, next they came from the north, and finally they are coming from the south in the exact order as foretold in Isaiah.

The nation of Israel will never again be two nations or be divided into two kingdoms. After Solomon's rule, the 12 tribes of Israel spilt into two nations, Israel (10 tribes) and Judah (two tribes). Until the two nations were scattered, they lived in constant disagreement and strife. In 1948 when the state of Israel was reborn, this tribal division failed to be reinstituted. This was according to God's word: "I will take the Israelites out of the nations where they have gone. I will gather them from all around and bring them back into their own land. I will make them one nation in the land, on the mountains of Israel. There will be one king over all of them and they will never again be two nations or be divided into two kingdoms."

Jesus is to return when the Jewish people go back to a common language so that they may call upon the name of the Lord, to serve Him with one consent. In the 19th century, modern Hebrew was revived as a spoken language and replaced Arabic, Yiddish, Russian, and a variety of other languages spoken by Jewish people who immigrated to Israel. In 1948, it became the official language of the newly declared State of Israel. The return of the Hebrew language to regular usage is miraculous; there are no other examples of a language (devoid of native speakers) becoming a national language with millions of first-language speakers in such a short amount of time.

Jesus will return when people shall call upon His name seek His face. In 1998, there were only about 3,500 Messianic Jewish people (Jewish believers in

Jesus) and 80 congregations in Israel.29 In 2008, there were believed to be about 10,000 to 15,000 Jewish believers and 120 congregations. However, it is difficult to accurately determine the number of Messianic Jewish folks in Israel because many are reluctant to be public about their views due to severe persecution by the Orthodox Jewish people. Nevertheless, increasing numbers are accepting their Messiah every day. The more people who call on God's name, the closer we will be to His second coming.

When the Jewish people return home, God will restore their fortunes. Israel is becoming one of the richest nations. In a 2007/2008 report by the United Nations Development Programme, Israel ranked 23rd in gross national product per capita annual growth rate from 1990 to 2005.30 Cut diamonds, technology, and agricultural products (fruits and vegetables) are the leading exports. Israel has been compared to the Silicon Valley in its development of cutting-edge technologies in software, communications, and the life sciences.

You will hear of wars and rumors of wars, but see to it that you are not alarmed. Is this not true every evening on the nightly news? Although we are faced with this daily, we have become numb to perilous times.

The building of the Third Temple and the seeking of the Red Heifer are underway. The Temple Institute is dedicated to building the Third Temple. So far, virtually all the instruments that will be used in the temple have been precisely recreated. The Third Temple will be built before Jesus returns for His people. The sacrifice of the Red Heifer and the resultant ashes are needed for the ritual purification of a priest for temple service; a Red Heifer is a necessary prerequisite for participating in any service in the temple. Only nine Red Heifers were actually slaughtered in the period extending from Moses to the destruction of the Second Temple. According to Jewish oral traditions and literature, the tenth red heifer will be sacrificed by the Messiah. Today, efforts are being made to build the temple and locate a Red Heifer for the Messiah's return.

ial gospel of Jesus will be preached all over the world as a witness to all the nations, and then the end will come. With the advent of the printing press and the translation of the Bible into over 2,300 languages and dialects (covering over 90% of the world's population), people can obtain their own copy of the Bible and read it for themselves. Furthermore, using modern communication, the gospel is being preached around the world via radio, television, Internet, missionaries, and more. Satellites are beaming the gospel into even the most remote areas and the most anti-Christian countries on earth.

Information and transportation will increase in the last days. For thousands of years until as recent as 150 years ago, the fastest mode of transportation was on horseback. Today, mankind can travel over 25,000 mph and all the way to the moon. Mass transportation systems can move millions of people each day. In regard to the increase in information, we live in the Information Age. With the use of computers and the Internet, information and knowledge exchange is exponentially increasing every year. Even the most skeptical mind must admit that knowledge is exploding in all directions. It has been estimated that 80% percent of the world's total knowledge has been brought forth in the last decade.

There will be signs in the sun, moon, and stars; the sea and the waves will roar; earthquakes will shake the earth in various places. Over the past decade, we have witnessed several natural disasters, many in the form of water (i.e., floods and hurricanes). In the Book of Revelation, water floods out of the mouth of the beast. Perhaps the excessive flooding today is a sign of the rising antichrist. Furthermore, a 2008 earthquake cracked the temple mount in Jerusalem.

The wasteland will be reclaimed and the desert will bloom. Israel is effectively using irrigation to return the dry desert wasteland to a lush garden. Their efforts are so successful that the country's border is called the Green Line because there is such a distinct demarcation between Israel and the surrounding countries. One of Israel's greatest exports is fruits and vegetables.

As described in the book of Ezekiel, the Dead Sea will be split into fresh and salt portions. This prophecy in underway. The sea has indeed split; however, the difference in salinity of the water is yet to come. The Israelis are proposing a canal between the Red Sea and the Dead Sea. It is postulated that the canal could increase the seismic activity of the region and the salt composition of the Dead Sea.

And it shall come to pass afterward, that God will pour out His spirit upon all flesh; and our sons and daughters will prophesy, old men will dream dreams, and young men will see visions. Ask spirit-filled Christians today and they will tell you that there has been an increase in the number of prophetic dreams and visions in their life.

End-Time Events in the Book of Revelation

In the Book of Revelation, John describes what he saw when he was called to Heaven to witness the end times. It is important to note that the sequence and timing of the events are somewhat uncertain because time doesn't exist in Heaven like it does on earth. In general, the book is divided into sevens: seven letters to the churches, seven seals, seven trumpets, and seven bowls. The seven letters warn the churches of the end times. In the end-time events, the seven seals are followed by the seven trumpets, which in turn are followed by the seven bowls of wrath.

While in Heaven, John saw a scroll with seven seals in the right hand of the Lord. An angel asked who was worthy to open the scroll, but no one in Heaven or on earth could open the scroll or even look inside it. When John began to weep, an elder said, "Do not weep! See, the Lion of the tribe of Judah, the Root of David, has triumphed. He is able to open the scroll and its seven seals."[31]

Then John saw the Lamb of God take the scroll and the twenty-four elders began to sing a new song.

> *You are worthy to take the scroll, and to open its seals; for You were slain, and have redeemed us to God by Your blood out of every tribe and tongue and people and nation, and have made us kings and priests to our God; and we shall reign on the earth.* (Rev. 5:9-10 NIV)

THE BIG PICTURE

Relative Timeline of Events in John's Revelation

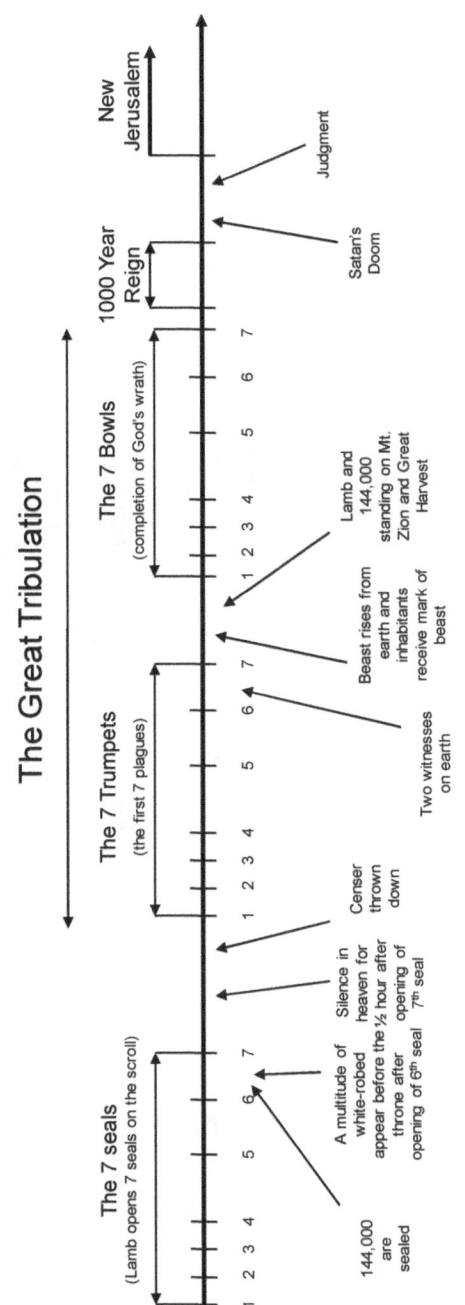

The Short Version
According to John's Revelation

- The first six seals are opened, but the consequences of the first four are held back until the sealing of the 144,000 Jews on earth and the rapture of the redeemed into Heaven.

- After the sixth seal and before the seventh, the 144,000 are sealed and the redeemed are raptured.

- The seventh seal is broken and there is silence in Heaven for half an hour. Then, the angel throws to earth the censer filled with fire from the altar and the seven trumpets (a warning and a call to repentance) begin.

- First six trumpets blow and the consequences occur.

- After sixth trumpet, the 144,000 Jews are joined with Christ on Mt. Zion and then there is a Great Harvest of those people who turned to God and didn't take the mark of the beast. At this point, there are no more believers on earth.

- The seventh trumpet proclaims the Kingdom of God and is followed by the seven bowls of God's wrath.

- The seven bowls of wrath are poured out on the people who refused to accept God and who worshipped the beast instead. These bowls contain God's vengeance on these people.

- After the wrath is finished, Babylon is destroyed and the beast and his army are cast into Hell while Jesus reigns for 1000 years.

- At the end of the 1000 years, the beast is released for one last chance at repentance. Instead he mounts an attack against God and His people. The beast is bound and he and his army are cast into Hell for eternity.

- God judges all people at the Great White Throne Judgment.

- God restores the earth and brings down New Jerusalem where the redeemed will live with Him forever.

Seven Seals

The scroll that originates from the throne of God *in Heaven* has seven seals that are opened *in Heaven* by Jesus Christ; however, most of the events (except the fifth seal) happen *on earth*.

The seven seals (see **Table 1**) are not a part of the contents of the scroll, but in fact are conditions to its opening. Furthermore, the opening of a seal is not contingent upon completing what was designated by a previous seal. In other words, the opening of the third seal does not depend upon the completion of the events in the second seal.

The first four of the seven seals are commonly referred to as the Four Horsemen or the Four Horses of the Apocalypse. These four horses are not unique to the Book of Revelation. Zechariah, who saw four horses of the same color, was told that they represent the four spirits of Heaven that stand in the presence of the Lord of the whole world. He saw the black horse go north, the white horse go west, the pale horse go south, and the red horse (by inference) go west. These spirits (often thought of as senior angels) go throughout the earth at God's command to accomplish His will.

Table 1. Events After the Opening of the Seven Seals

1st Seal (The Conqueror)	A rider with a bow on a white horse will be given a crown and he will ride out as a conqueror bent on conquest.
2nd Seal (Conflict on Earth)	A rider with a large sword on a fiery red horse will be given power to take peace from the earth and to make men slay each other.

3rd Seal (Scarcity on Earth)	A rider on a black horse will appear holding a pair of scales in his hand.
4th Seal (Widespread Death on Earth)	Two riders, Death on a pale horse and Hades following closely behind, will be given power over a fourth of the earth to kill by sword, famine, plague, and by the wild beasts of the earth.
5th Seal (The Cry of the Martyrs)	John saw under the altar the souls of those who had been slain because of the word of God and their testimony. They will be given a white robe and told to wait a little longer until the number of their fellow servants and brothers who were to be killed as they had been is completed.
6th Seal (Cosmic Disturbances)	There will be a great earthquake. The sun will turn black and the whole moon will turn blood red. The stars in the sky will fall to earth and the sky will recede like a scroll rolling up. Every mountain and island will be removed from their place.
7th Seal (Prelude to the Seven Trumpets)	There will be silence in Heaven for approximately half an hour.

When the fifth seal is opened, the martyrs under the altar will begin to cry out. They will be given a white robe and told to wait a little longer. After the opening of the sixth seal, a great earthquake will shake the earth. The sun will turn black and the whole moon will turn blood red. The stars in the sky will fall to earth and the sky will recede like a scroll rolling up. Every mountain and island will be removed from its place. Not surprisingly, everyone will seek shelter and try to hide.

Then, John saw four angels standing at the four corners of the earth, holding the four winds of the earth. Before the four horsemen are permitted to conduct their mission, 144,000 Jewish people will be sealed and the redeemed will be raptured.

Sealing of 144,000 Jewish People

John saw an angel ascending from the east and having the seal of the living God. The angel cried with a loud voice to the four apocalyptic angels, "Do not harm the earth, the sea, or the trees until we have sealed the servants of our God on their foreheads." One hundred and forty-four thousand (12,000 from each tribe of Israel) will be sealed. They will be left on earth to witness and be an example through the tribulation period, in great similarity to when the Israelites were in Egypt. Although the Egyptians were ridden with plagues, the Israelites were not touched. The Lord will make a distinction between His people and the world. John sees these 144,000 people later riding with Jesus.

Rapture of the Redeemed

After the sealing of the 144,000, John saw a great innumerable multitude (from all nations, tribes, peoples, and tongues) standing before the throne of God and Jesus. They were clothed with white robes, holding palm branches in their hands, and crying out with a loud voice, "Salvation belongs to our God who sits on the throne, and to the Lamb!"32

An elder asked John if he knew who these people were or from where they had come. When John couldn't answer, the elder proceeded to explain: "These are the ones who come out of the great tribulation, and washed their robes and made them white in the blood of the Lamb. They are before the throne of God, and serve Him day and night. He who sits on the throne will dwell among them, and they shall neither hunger nor thirst anymore. The Lamb who is in the midst of the throne will shepherd them and lead them to living fountains of waters, and God will wipe away every tear from their eyes."33

So, who really are the redeemed? They are those who have accepted Jesus Christ as their Savior and Redeemer; they will be saved and will have eternal life in the presence of Almighty God. Their old self was crucified with Jesus so that the body of sin might be done away with, that they should no longer be slaves to sin. The blood of Jesus washed away their sin and inequities, and they wear the white robe of righteousness. If they have accepted the blood of Jesus, then they will be redeemed.

Seven Trumpets

After the opening of the seventh seal, there will be silence in Heaven for half an hour as a solemn reverence of the opening of the seven seals and the yet-to-come blowing of the seven trumpets.

Seven angels will each be given a trumpet, while another angel with a golden censer will come and stand at the altar. John saw the angel receive incense to offer with the prayers of all the saints upon the golden altar that was before the throne. The smoke of the incense, with the prayers of the saints, ascended before God from the angel's hand. Then the angel took the censer, filled it with fire from the altar, and hurled it on the earth. Afterward, there came peals of thunder, rumblings, flashes of lightning, and an

THE BIG PICTURE

earthquake. The seven angels who had the seven trumpets prepared themselves to sound.

These seven trumpets, which resemble the plagues upon Egypt, will be sent to warn mankind and to call mankind to repentance (see **Table 2**). They are designed to arrest the attention of the world so that everyone can hear the gospel. In addition, the trumpets will create an environment that will sober every living person to the point at which they will at least consider the gospel. This proclamation of the gospel will attract everyone sincere in heart, but will powerfully repel those who rebel against God. Thus, they also serve to further divide the people before the Great Harvest.

Table 2. Events After the Sounding of the Seven Trumpets

1st Trumpet (Vegetation Struck)	Hail and fire mixed with blood will be hurled down upon the earth. A third of the earth, a third of the trees, and all the green grass will be burned up.
2nd Trumpet (Seas Struck)	Something like a huge mountain on fire will be thrown into the sea. A third of the sea will be turned into blood, a third of the living creatures in the sea will die, and a third of the ships will be destroyed.
3rd Trumpet (Waters Struck)	A great star, blazing like a torch, will fall from the sky on a third of the rivers and springs of water. A third of the waters will turn bitter causing many people to die.
4th Trumpet (Heavens Struck)	A third of the sun will be struck, a third of the moon, and a third of the stars, so that a third of them will turn dark. A third of the day will be without light, and also a third of the night.

5th Trumpet (Locusts From the Bottomless Pit)	An angel who will be given the key to the shaft of the abyss will fall to the earth and open the abyss. The sun and sky will be darkened by the smoke rising from the abyss. Out of the smoke will come scorpion-like locusts that will be instructed to harm only those people who do not have the seal of God on their foreheads. The creatures will not be given power to kill the people, but only to torture them for five months.
6th Trumpet (Angels From the Euphrates)	The four angels who are bound at the great river Euphrates and who have been kept ready for this very hour will be released to kill mankind. A third of mankind will be killed by the three plagues of fire, smoke, and sulfur that will come from their mouths.
7th Trumpet (Kingdom Proclaimed)	The twenty-four elders, who will be seated on their thrones before God, will fall on their faces and worship. Then God's temple in Heaven will be opened, and within His temple will be seen the ark of His covenant. And there will come flashes of lightning, rumblings, thunder, an earthquake, and a great hailstorm.

The Two Witnesses

Between the sixth and seventh trumpets, the Lord will give His power to two witnesses and they will prophesy for 1,260 days and call mankind to repentance. They will have the power to stop the rains, turn waters to blood, and to strike the earth with every kind of plague. Anyone who tries to harm them will be devoured by fire from their mouths.

When the witnesses have finished their testimony, the beast that comes up from the abyss will kill them. Afterward, their bodies will lie in the city streets, and for three and a half days everyone will gaze upon their bodies and refuse to bury them. However, after the three and a half days, breath of life from God will enter them and they will stand to their feet. They will be caught up to Heaven in a cloud, while their enemies look on. At that very hour, there will be a severe earthquake and a tenth of the city will collapse.

The two witnesses are believed to be Enoch and Elijah who had not yet experienced death. Enoch walked with God; then he was no more because God took him away. As Elijah and Elisha were walking along and talking together, suddenly a chariot of fire and horses of fire appeared and separated the two of them, and Elijah went up to Heaven in a whirlwind.

The Return of Jesus Christ

During the sounding of the seventh trumpet, Jesus Christ will return. He will come down from Heaven with a loud command, with the voice of the archangel, and with the trumpet call of God. The loud voices in Heaven will say, "The kingdoms of this world have become the kingdoms of our Lord and of His Christ, and He shall reign forever and ever!"34 The twenty-four elders who sit before God on their thrones will fall on their faces and worship Him.

The Dragon and the Beasts

The Kingdom of Heaven is outside the realm of time. After the sounding of the seventh trumpet, John sees other events, like the fall of Lucifer and the rise of the beast. However, it is unlikely that these events are sequential with the trumpets because we know that Satan was on earth in the Garden. It is likely that John witnessed a sort of flashback of previous events to bring the situation up to speed for his understanding.

John saw the dragon (Satan) standing on the shore of the sea. Then he saw the rise of a beast from the sea. The dragon will give his power and authority to the beast. John saw that one of the heads of the beast had a fatal wound that had been healed. Let's stop here and consider this issue. If a wound is described as fatal, how could the beast be alive? His wound is an attempt to imitate the crucified Jesus. This beast is the antichrist—the mirror image of the crucified and resurrected Jesus. The whole world will be astonished at the beast and will follow him. He will blaspheme God and conquer the saints.

Then John saw a beast rising from the earth. He had two horns like a lamb (Jesus), but he spoke like a dragon. This could be a picture of a deceived high-ranking Christian, appearing to be one thing but sounding like another. This beast will perform great and miraculous signs, even causing fire to come down from Heaven to earth. Because of these signs and wonders, he will deceive the inhabitants of the earth. He also will force everyone, small and great, rich and poor, free and slave, to receive a mark (which is the name of the beast or the number of his name) on his right hand or on his forehead, so that no one will be able to buy or sell unless he has the mark.

The beast, dragon, and the false prophet (who performs miraculous signs on the beast's behalf) are representative of the satanic version of the Holy Trinity.

The Great Harvest of the Earth

Before the earth was harvested of those who were saved, John saw the 144,000 Jewish people who had been redeemed from the earth standing with Jesus on Mount Zion. They will be singing a song that only they can sing. They are the ones who did not defile themselves and kept themselves pure. They will follow the Lamb wherever He goes. They were purchased from among men and offered as first fruits to God and the Lamb. The remnant of Israel will do no wrong; they will speak no lies, nor will deceit be found in their mouths. They will eat and lie down and no one will make them afraid.

Then John saw three angels in the air. The first angel will proclaim the eternal gospel to those on the earth. The second angel will follow and say, "Fallen! Fallen is Babylon the Great, which made all the nations drink the maddening wine of her adulteries." And, the third angel will say in a loud voice, "If anyone worships the beast and his image and receives his mark on the forehead or on the hand, he too will drink of the wine of God's fury, which has been poured full strength into the cup of his wrath. He will be tormented with burning sulfur in the presence of the holy angels and of the Lamb. And the smoke of their torment rises forever and ever. There is no rest day or night for those who worship the beast and his image, or for anyone who receives the mark of his name."35

There before John was a white cloud, and seated on the cloud was one like a son of man with a crown of gold on his head and a sharp sickle in his hand. Another angel came out of the temple and called in a loud voice to him who was sitting on the cloud, "Take your sickle and reap, because the time to reap has come, for the harvest of the earth is ripe."36 So He who was seated on the cloud will swing His sickle over the earth, and the earth will be harvested of the redeemed.

The Seven Bowls of God's Wrath

John then saw seven angels having the seven last plagues—last because with these plagues, God's wrath will be completed. The seven bowls are actually seven pay-backs for those who received the mark of the beast (see **Table 3**). Ultimately, the purpose of the seven last plagues is vengeance.

The seven plagues have been compared to God's warnings given in Leviticus:

*If after all this you will not listen to me, I will punish you for your sins seven times over.37

*If you remain hostile toward me and refuse to listen to me, I will multiply your afflictions seven times over, as your sins deserve.38

*If in spite of these things you do not accept my correction but continue to be hostile toward me, I myself will be hostile toward you and will afflict you for your sins seven times over.39

*If in spite of this you still do not listen to me but continue to be hostile toward me, then in my anger I will be hostile toward you, and I myself will punish you for your sins seven times over.40

Unlike the trumpets, the bowls are not warnings; they are God's long-suffering wrath. They will follow a similar pattern as the seven trumpets: four affecting creation

THE BIG PICTURE

(earth, sea, water, cosmos); two associated with the beast or man; and the final one directed toward the nations.

The seventh bowl will directly follow the sixth bowl. There will be no interlude like with the six and seventh seals and trumpets. These pauses will provide a time for witnessing and reflecting upon the gospel. During the pouring of the bowls of wrath, the time for repentance will be long past.

During the seven bowls, God will release His wrath on Babylon. John witnessed the fall of this nation, as well as the world's mourning and Heaven's rejoicing.

Table 3. Events After the Seven Bowls of Wrath

1st Bowl (Loathsome Sores)	The first angel will pour out his bowl on the land, and ugly and painful sores will break out on the people who have the mark of the beast and who worship his image.
2nd Bowl (Sea Turns to Blood)	The second angel will pour out his bowl on the sea, and it will be turned into blood, and every living thing in the sea will die.
3rd Bowl (Water Turns to Blood)	The third angel will pour out his bowl on the rivers and springs of water, and they will become blood.
4th Bowl (Men Are Scorched)	The fourth angel will pour out his bowl on the sun, which will be given power to scorch people with fire.
5th Bowl (Darkness and Pain)	The fifth angel will pour out his bowl on the throne of the beast, and his kingdom will be plunged into darkness.
6th Bowl (Euphrates Dried Up)	The sixth angel will pour out his bowl on the great river Euphrates, and its water will be dried up. Then three evil spirits will come out of the dragon, the beast, and the false prophet. These

	spirits of demons will perform miraculous signs, and they will gather the kings at Armageddon for the great battle.
7th Bowl (Earth Shaken)	The seventh angel will pour out his bowl into the air, and out of the temple will come a loud voice from the throne, saying, "It is done!" Then will come flashes of lightning, rumblings, thunder, and a severe earthquake. The great city will be split into three parts, and the cities of the nations will collapse. From the sky huge hailstones of about a hundred pounds each will fall upon men.

The Thousand Years

After the seventh bowl, a rider called Faithful and True on a white horse will appear wearing a robe dipped in blood. On His robe and thigh, His name will be written: KING OF KINGS AND LORD OF LORDS. His name is the Word of God. The armies of Heaven will be following Him, riding on white horses and dressed in clean, white linen. Out of His mouth will come a sharp sword to strike down the nations.

The rider and His army will capture the beast and the false prophet and throw them alive into the fiery lake of burning sulfur. The rest of beast's army will be killed with the sword that comes out of the mouth of the rider on the horse. An angel from Heaven, holding the key to the abyss and a great chain, will seize the dragon (the ancient serpent) and bind him for a thousand years in the abyss to keep him from deceiving the nations. After that, he will be set free for a short time.

John then saw seated on the thrones those who have been given the authority to judge. He saw the ones who had died because they had not worshiped the beast or his image and had not received his mark. They will come to life and reign with Christ for the thousand years. (This is the first resurrection. The rest of the dead will not come to life until the thousand years have ended.)

Satan's Doom

When the thousand years are over, Satan will be released from his prison and allowed to deceive the nations of the earth and to gather them for battle. They will march across the earth and surrounded the camp of God's people. However, fire will come down from Heaven and devour them, and the devil will be thrown into the lake of burning sulfur, where the antichrist and the false prophet have already been thrown. They will be tormented day and night forever and ever.

The prophet Isaiah foretold of Satan's doom:

> *But you are cast out of your grave like an abominable branch, like the garment of those who are slain, thrust through with a sword, who go down to the stones of the pit, like a corpse trodden underfoot. You will not be joined with them in burial, because you have destroyed your land and slain your people. The offspring of the wicked will never be mentioned again.* (Is. 14:19-20 NKJV)

The Great White Throne Judgment

Then John saw a great white throne and He who was seated on it. He saw the dead, great and small, standing before the throne. The sea will give up the dead that are in it, and death and Hades will give up the dead that are in them. John saw books, including the Book of Life, open.

The dead will be judged according to what they have done as recorded in the books. Each person will be judged according to what he has done. If anyone's name is not found written in the Book of Life, he will be thrown into the lake of fire with Satan and his demons.

The Old Testament continually references God's call of the Israelites to repentance and warns them of His impending judgment. The texts from Joel, Isaiah, Ezekiel, Zechariah, and Malachi all speak of a universal judgment at the end time in apocalyptic contexts. Specifically, Joel predicts a universal judgment on the nations. The apocalyptic end-time judgment is also clearly presented in Isaiah, Chapters 24 through 27, frequently called the Isaiah Apocalypse.

Jesus stated that God did not send Him into the world to judge the world, but that the world should be saved through Him. Whoever believes in Him is not condemned, but whoever does not believe stands condemned already, because he has not believed in the name of God's one and only Son. This does not mean that Jesus will not judge the world; He just won't do it until He comes again.

So, who exactly will be judged? The Bible says we all must appear before the judgment seat of Christ, that each one may receive what is due him for the things done while in the body, whether good or bad. Ecclesiastes emphasizes that God will judge both the righteous man and the wicked man. Thus, all human beings, regardless of whether they are righteous or wicked, will be judged by God. The Lord says that for His flock, He will judge between one sheep and another, between the rams and the male goats.

By what will we be judged? The standard of judgment will be the Word of God. Our faith and works recorded in the heavenly books will be measured accordingly against this standard. These books are mentioned several times in the Old Testament. In the Book of Daniel, it is written: The court was seated, and the books were opened. These circumstances indicate some sort of investigation during the heavenly judgment session.

The measuring rod of the judgment will be God's law. All who have sinned under the law will be judged by the law. Even Gentiles, who do not have the law, will be judged by the law, because it has been written upon their conscience and they strive to uphold it. However, no matter how hard you strive to uphold the law or be a good person, you will fail. Jesus was the only being who lived on earth and was without sin. He was a pure and acceptable sacrifice under which we are no longer slaves to the law. If we have accepted Him as our redeemer, we will still be judged by the law; however, we will be found righteous because we have been washed clean in His sacrificial blood. Salvation is only through Jesus our Savior.

Paul states in Romans that not the hearers of the law are just before God, but the doers of the law shall be justified. It is not enough to be a knower and respecter of the law; one must also be a doer. It is clear that we will be judged by what we do. In 1st Corinthians, it states that our work will be shown for what it is. Its quality will be revealed and tested with fire. If our works survive, we will receive a reward; if they are burned up, we will suffer a loss. We will be saved, but only as one escaping through the flames. The idea that judgment is according to works is repeated in 2nd Corinthians, which states that we will be recompensed for our deeds. However, the Bible clearly states that *by grace* we have been saved, *through faith* in Jesus Christ. Not by works, so that no one can boast, and not from ourselves, but as a gift from God. So which is it? Are we saved by works or by faith?

The answer is neither and both, at the very same time. True biblical faith is not passive. Our works demonstrate our spiritual maturity. We are to live a life of faith and also to produce works by faith. Consider Abraham when he offered his son Isaac on the altar. You see that his faith and his actions were working together; his faith was made complete by his actions. Works without faith are dead, just as faith with works is dead. Ultimately, though, we are saved by our confession and faith in salvation through Jesus Christ and this will be our admission ticket to heaven. When we get there, our reward will be based on the judgment of our works.

Eternal Life or Eternal Death

God's master plan ends with man sharing eternal life with Him. John witnessed all things being made new. The Holy City, the New Jerusalem, will come down out of Heaven. God will dwell with his people forever. There will be no more death, mourning, crying, or pain. No longer will there be any curse of sin. Once again, man will abide with God like he did in the Garden. Only this time, it will be for eternity. There will be a great joy of the redeemed as the prophet Isaiah foretold in Chapter 35:

*The desert and land will rejoice and blossom.
*Blind will see.
*Deaf will hear.
*Lame will leap like deer.
*Mute will shout for joy.
*Water will gush forth.

*There will be no ravenous beasts.

*Only the redeemed will walk there and the ransomed of the Lord will return.

*Everlasting joy will crown our heads.

*There will be no sorrow or sighing.

God never intended for any of mankind to live eternally apart from Him. Nevertheless, there will be people who will refuse the gift of salvation, even in the midst of the end-time fury. Everyone who rejects God will experience eternal death, as opposed to eternal life. They will be put to shame and will be written in the dust.

Jesus spoke of eternal death in His parable of the wedding banquet. Everyone who refused the invitation to the banquet was directed by the king to be bound by hand and foot, taken away, and cast into outer darkness. He said there will be weeping and gnashing of teeth, for many are called, but few are chosen.

In another passage in the Bible, the place of eternal punishment is described as the place where the worm does not die and the fire is not quenched. It is everlasting destruction and absence from the Lord and from the majesty of His power. Instead, eternal death will be in the fiery pits of Hell with Satan and all his demons.

Chapter 8
THE BIG PICTURE IN A NUTSHELL

In 100 words:

God created man in His image for fellowship. He didn't create man as a perfect being initially (because only God is perfect, and He would have just created Himself, had He created perfection), so God designed a purification process whereby man would attain holiness. When man fell into sin, which brought about the consequence of death, God set forth a Redeemer to stand in place of man for death. By this, the sin of man would die with the replacement, and man would be permitted to live forever with God, thus achieving God's initial goal of having an eternal family.

Old vs New Testaments

Many folks simply do not see the ties between the Old Testament and the New Testament, while others don't believe that there is a tie because several thousand years separate the two testaments. Also, the written tones of each testament are different.

Tone differences are inevitable. In the Old Testament, times were tough. Imagine all the luxuries we have today and how this greatly contrasts with the world of one

THE BIG PICTURE

hundred years ago. Now imagine how tough things would have been thousands of years ago. Oppression ran rampant, and survival was a struggle in daily life. Today, people struggle with issues like which type of specialty coffee to choose for their morning drive.

By the time of the New Testament, many conveniences were available due to the construction ingenuity and resourcefulness of the Romans and Greeks. For example, consider the grand coliseums and plumbing and water supply mechanisms, which were somewhat rudimentary yet existent—things that were unimaginable in the times of the Old Testament.

The Old Testament is perceived to be about an angry, jealous god who continually pours out his wrath on the people; whereas, in the New Testament, Jesus is seen as a loving and patient being. In reality, our God is the same yesterday, today, and forever. He never changes, although our perception of Him does.

God in the Old Testament times was just as loving and patient as Jesus. Sure, He killed many people, sometimes for things we perceive as trivial, but you must keep in mind the bigger picture. He loved creation so much that He would do almost anything to preserve it and bring to fruition His master plan. He set aside a sect of people whom He could shield and protect from the rest of the world. This nation of Israel had a very special role in God's redemption plan. First, He used them to deliver the Law and to reveal sin to man. Then, He had to keep them from falling into the world system in order to keep a chosen bloodline through which the Redeemer would arise.

Despite His continual forgiveness and persistent warnings, the Jewish people just could not hold it together.

They repeatedly fell away from God, and each time He had to take drastic measures to bring them back in line. Imagine trying to keep a thousand marbles from rolling off a table that tilts, twists, and turns. This is a picture of God hovering over His people, trying to herd them like little chicks. It is a picture of great love and enduring patience.

For all those folks who constantly reject God because they can't believe that a god of love would permit such atrocities like innocent children with fatal diseases—get a clue!!! There is more to the picture than we can even imagine. Our eyes are limited by light frequencies and other physiological factors, and we can't fully see what is truly around us. Let alone, we can't read a single person's thoughts or heart. But God can do this. He knows all, sees all. How dare we think we know enough of the story to judge God's intentions!

Everyone always remembers Jesus, on the other hand, for His gentleness. We picture Him sitting under a tree with small children camped all around as He enjoys their company, or we envision Him standing patiently and knocking at a door as we have seen in so many paintings. Jesus is all these things and more. However, He wasn't always the nice, politically correct guy. He had a habit of calling people out, especially the Pharisees and Sadducees. At times, He showed irritation at the disciples' constant lack of faith despite all the miracles they had witnessed. Or how about when He stormed the outer courts of the temple, made a whip out of cords, and drove out everyone and all the animals; He scattered the coins of the money changers and overturned their tables. Not exactly His most gentle moment.

Importance of the Feasts

God said that the Jewish people are to appear before Him and to celebrate a festival dedicated to Him. He ordained several feasts for the Israelites to observe. The purpose of theses feasts was threefold: 1) to honor and thank God; 2) to remember what He brought them through; and 3) to prepare them for the Messiah and the end times (a rehearsal of sorts). A religious festival, a New Moon celebration, or a Sabbath day—these were a shadow of the things that were to come.

During each feast, no one was to appear before God empty-handed. Most times, an animal sacrifice was to be made. While God made some animals and birds with His words, He made others out of the ground like Adam. (Perhaps the origination of the animal or bird determined whether it was clean or unclean. Noah had to take seven of every kind of clean animal and two of every kind of unclean animal onto the Ark.) It's been postulated that the creatures He made out of the ground were the ones used in sacrifices to stand in the gap for man. That is why they were made from the same substance. Animals were used because they know no sin; they are sinless offerings.

The animal sacrifice itself was very bloody and gory. It was not intended to be neat, but instead was meant to make a lasting impression on the person performing it. Basically, the person sacrificing the animal had to cut the animal's throat with one hand as he held the restrained animal with the other. He had to look into its eyes as he took its life. No doubt, this strong and off-putting action was a deterrent to sin.

Following is a list of the seven feasts instituted by God.

*Passover

*Feast of Unleavened Bread

*First Fruits

*Feast of Weeks (Pentecost, the Feast of Harvest, or Shavuot)

*Feast of Trumpets (Rosh Hashanah)

*Day of Atonement (Yom Kippur)

*Feast of Tabernacles (Feast of the Ingathering)

The feasts follow a pattern of seasons (sowing, harvesting, etc), a pattern of spiritual states (ie, Spring = deliverance, Summer = preparation, Fall = repentance), and a pattern of God's plan for the Israelites (exodus, giving of law, etc). The Jewish people use two kinds of calendars: a civil calendar used for childbirth, contracts, and such, and a religious calendar used for computing the religious festivals and to determine which Torah portions to read each day. The sacred year comes from original directives given to Moses.

Passover and the Feast of Unleavened Bread

Passover is commemoration of God's deliverance of the Israelites and of their separation from Egypt. When the Israelites were oppressed in Egypt and the Pharaoh would not let them leave, God instructed Moses to have all the Israelites take blood from a lamb without defect and apply it to their doorpost. The Israelites were to remain in their houses, under the covering of the blood. When the Lord passed through that night, He struck the firstborn of every house unless the blood was applied. As a result, the Pharaoh ordered the Israelites to leave Egypt, as they wished.

The Israelites were to celebrate this event every year as a reminder of what the Lord had done for them. The Passover was a blood covenant in which blood from a sinless lamb would be payment for death. The Passover lamb was to be killed between the evenings (translated as about 3:00 pm, or the ninth hour).

Passover is the first day of the Feast of Unleavened Bread. For seven days the Israelites were to eat bread made without yeast. Leaven represents sin in one's heart and life, and thus this feast was a reminder to live one's life without sin.

Feast of First Fruits

The Feast of First Fruits is the only Levitical feast no longer observed in modern Judaism. It was originally a commemoration of God's provision for His people. The Israelites were to celebrate with the first fruits of the crops sown in the field. Today, the Feast of First Fruits is celebrated by Christians and is otherwise known as Easter.

Feast of Weeks

Fifty days after Passover begins is the Feast of Weeks, also known as Pentecost, the Feast of Harvest, or Shavuot. According to Rabbinic tradition, the Ten Commandments were given on this day. This feast was a commemoration of God's provision of the Law. As part of the sacrifice, a wave offering of two loaves of bread made with leaven (representing sin) was to be done. This is the only offering in which leaven was allowed. All other offerings were to be sinless.

Feast of Trumpets

The Feast of Trumpets (Rosh Hashanah) is the commemoration of a New Year. It is announced by the blowing of trumpets, which is also a call to the Israelite community for assembly. At Rosh Hashanah, the shofar sounds in Synagogues all over the world. The sound of the trumpet is a reminder of the grace God granted Abraham when He supplied him with a sacrificial ram to replace his son Isaac.

Day of Atonement

The Day of Atonement (Yom Kippur) is a commemoration of the need for atonement. It is preceded by the Ten Days of Awe and is a period of repentance initiated by the sounding of the trumpet on Rosh Hashanah. During the Ten Days of Awe, the Israelites are to consider their ways and turn their hearts toward God. A change of heart must first take place before the redeeming sacrifices of Yom Kippur can be accepted.

According to tradition, Yom Kippur is considered the date on which Moses received the second set of Ten Commandments. At this same time, the Israelites were granted atonement for the sin of the Golden Calf. Jewish people have traditionally observed this holiday with a twenty-four hour period of fasting and intensive prayer. Most of the holiday is spent praying in the Synagogue. God mandates that anyone who does not observe the regulations on this day must be cut off from his people.

Feast of Tabernacles

The Feast of Tabernacles (Feast of Ingathering or Sukkot) is a commemoration of the Israelite history. This festival lasts for seven days, with the first and eighth days being days of rest. As prescribed in the Bible, all native-born Israelites were to live in booths so the descendants would know that God had the Israelites live in tents when He brought them out of Egypt. Today, the religious Jewish people live in a Sukkah (or tabernacle) to honor the time when Israel lived in tents during their forty years in the desert.

The Feast of Tabernacles is a drastic transition from one of the most solemn holidays in the Jewish year (Yom Kippur, or the Day of Atonement) to one of the most joyous. The festival is so joyful that it is commonly referred to as the season of rejoicing.

During earlier times, the high point of the celebration was the "drawing of water" ceremony when the people called upon the Lord to provide heavenly waters for their next harvest season. A grand event that was full of much pomp and drama, it reached its peak on the last day of Sukkot, at which time the priests filled a golden pitcher with water from the pool of Siloam and returned to the temple.

****

Not only were the feasts rehearsals for the coming of the Messiah, but they were also a foreshadowing of the end-time events. The feasts were and are an integral part of the big picture. When considering both the trees and the entire forest of God's plan, the feasts are like the footpaths we follow.

The feasts were prophesies of Jesus and the Holy Spirit.

*Passover and Feast of Unleavened Bread was prophecy of the sinless offering of Christ. Jesus was the ultimate Passover lamb. He died when Passover lamb of the feast was sacrificed (the ninth hour), but unlike the festival lamb, the blood of Jesus is an eternal covering of all who come under it.

*The Feast of First Fruits was a prophecy of the resurrection of Christ. Christ has indeed been raised from the dead and is the first fruit.

*The Feast of Weeks (Pentecost) was a prophecy of the coming of the Holy Spirit. The two loaves of bread to be presented as a wave offering were to be made with leaven (representative of sin). The loaves could represent Jews and Gentiles brought together as one in Jesus Christ.

*The Feast of Trumpets is a prophecy of the second coming of Christ. The trumpets will announce the second coming of Jesus, who will descend from Heaven with a loud command, with the voice of the archangel, and with the trumpet call of God.

*The Day of Atonement is a prophecy of future redemption through the death and resurrection of Jesus Christ. There will be a redemption of Israel and a redemption of creation.

*The Feast of Tabernacles is a prophecy of God dwelling eternally with man. It points to a future Sukkot. On the last day of the feast, at the time of the drawing of water ceremony, Jesus stood and said, "If anyone is thirsty, let him come to me and drink. Whoever believes in me, will have streams

THE BIG PICTURE

of living water flowing from within him."41 Jesus was describing a time when all provisions will be made.

****

The description of the feasts in Leviticus Chapters 23 through 27 parallels the end-time events.

*Passover and Feast of Unleavened Bread celebrate death passing over the sealed first born and the coming out of Egypt. Passover draws similarity to the sealing of the 144,000 Jewish people. Whereas, the Feast of Unleavened Bread is a celebration of the rapture of those who are sinless (washed clean in the Blood and thus without leaven).

*First Fruits and the Feast of Weeks are similar to the events during the opening of the seven seals. Jesus is first fruit of resurrection. During the period between the first fruits and the Feast of Weeks, the fields are worked and the crops are tended. The cultivation of souls in the end-time events begins with the opening of the seven seals.

*Feast of Trumpets is a proclamation of the Savior. The initial trumpet blast on Rosh Hashanah bears to mind the grace of God and calls people to repentance. In the end times, it announces the second coming of Jesus and also presents a call to repentance. For ten days after Rosh Hashanah (known as the Ten Days of Awe) the people repent. These ten days are like the next six trumpets blowing.

*On the Day of Atonement, following the Ten Days of Awe, the High Priest enters the Holy of Holies to make atonement for everyone. In the end times, Jesus returns as our High Priest and makes eternal atonement for us.

*Feast of Tabernacles is a celebration commemorating the dwelling with God. It is synonymous with the thousand-year reign of Christ. Both are pictures of man living with God in a temporary dwelling.

*In Leviticus, Chapter 24, the oil and bread is set before the Lord and the blasphemer is stoned. This is similar to the Great Judgment, where everyone is brought before the Lord. Satan is cast into Hell.

*Leviticus, Chapters 25 though 27, is parallel with eternity after judgment. The redeemed will be rewarded and dwell forever (the Sabbath year) with the Lord. Likewise, the disobedient will be punished evermore.

Importance of the Jewish People

It is important to understand that the Jewish people were chosen to be a vehicle and to herald God's plan. Through them, He brought forth the law by which all are judged. These people were also chosen to make the way for the Redeemer. The Lord says that all peoples on earth will be blessed through Israel.

There is a dangerous false doctrine called Replacement Theology that is based on the idea that God's New Covenant is with the Christians and the Christian Church (according

THE BIG PICTURE

to the Bible, the covenant is with the house of Israel and with the house of Judah42), and that it replaces God's Mosaic Covenant with Israel. Basically, this doctrine states that the Church replaced Israel, transferred all blessings to the Christians, and left all curses to the Jewish people, particularly the non-believing ones.

Just to be 100% clear, the Church has NOT replaced Israel. God chose the Jewish people as His people. If He is the same yesterday, today, and tomorrow, then why would He change His mind and replace Israel with the Church? When Paul addressed this issue he asked whether God had reject his people. He immediately answered with "By no means!" In the letter to Ephesus, Paul states that Gentiles are heirs together with Israel; they are members together of one body and sharers together in the promise in Christ Jesus. God has not forsaken His chosen. Even today, you can see evidence of Him restoring Israel.

We owe the Jewish people for the Bible, Jesus, and everything in between. Without them, the world would have been doomed to death. In the Bible, it states that because Gentiles have shared in the Jews' spiritual blessings, they owe it to the people to share material blessings. The Lord tells the Gentiles to comfort His people. We are to speak tenderly to Jerusalem and proclaim to her that her hard service has been completed, that her sin has been paid for, and that she has received from the Lord's hand double for all her sins. And for those who refuse to bless and comfort Israel, there are curses. The Lord says that He will bless those who bless Israel and curse those who curse her.

If you would like to sow an ever-producing seed in the Kingdom of God, give to His people. When you bless Israel and her people, you will reap a return that is almost unimaginable. (I have witnessed it myself.) Better yet, you will be walking in the will of the Lord.

The Parable of the Good Samaritan

When Jesus was asked how to attain eternal life, He told the parable of the Good Samaritan. When this story is decoded as it is in *Unlocking the Prophecy Code: Understanding Bible Mysteries in Types and Shadows* by Dr. Bryan Cutshall,43 we can see the big picture of God's plan.

On one occasion an expert in the law stood up to test Jesus. "Teacher, what must I do to inherit eternal life?"

"What is written in the Law?" Jesus replied. "How do you read it?"

He answered: "Love the Lord your God with all your heart, all your soul, all your strength, and all your mind; and love your neighbor as yourself."

"You have answered correctly," Jesus replied. "Do this and you will live."

But he wanted to justify himself, so he asked Jesus, "And who is my neighbor?"

In reply, Jesus said: "A certain man was going down from Jerusalem to Jericho, when he fell among thieves. They stripped him of his clothes, beat him and went away, leaving him half dead. A certain priest happened to be going down the same road, and when he saw the man, he passed by on the other side. Likewise, a Levite, when arrived at the place, came and looked, and passed by on the other side. But a certain Samaritan, as he traveled, came where the man was; and when he saw him, had compassion. He went to him and bandaged his wounds, pouring on oil and wine. Then he put the man on his own animal, took him to an inn, and took care of him. The next day when he departed, he took out two denarii and gave them to the innkeeper. 'Look after him,' he said, 'and when I return, I will reimburse you for any extra expense you may have.' Which of these three do you think was a neighbor to the man who fell into the hands of robbers?"

The expert in the law replied, "The one who had mercy on him."

Jesus told him, "Go and do likewise."

****

Jerusalem is the city of God, His dwelling place. In this story, it represents the Garden of Eden, where man lived with God. Jericho represents the world. When Satan tempted Jesus, he offered Him Jericho (the world) if He would worship him.

The man going down from Jerusalem to Jericho refers to the fall of man (and thus, the man in question was Adam). He left the Garden where he was given authority over all creation and went to a place where he was subject to Satan's rule. In addition, he lost the daily fellowship and presence of the Lord. He would no longer dwell with God, but would be separated from Him. Even in the temple where God would sit in the Holy of the Holies, man was still separated from Him by a curtain.

On the way from Jerusalem to Jericho, the certain man (Adam) was attacked by thieves who represent Satan and his demonic forces. Man was stripped of his clothes, beaten, and left half dead. His clothes symbolize Adam's authority and anointing from God. His wounds represent man's transgression. He was left half dead—physically alive, but spiritually dead due to sin. This is the state of fallen man.

When the certain priest from the story came down the road, he saw the man, but passed on the other side. This priest represents Moses. Through Moses, God gave the law to identify sin; however, the law could not remove sin. The certain priest had no means to help the man, so he passed by.

Then a Levite came down the road. The Levite could make atonement for sin (could temporarily cover it), but could not remove it and restore sinful man to God. Therefore, he couldn't help the man either, so he passed by too.

But then there came a certain Samaritan. A Samaritan is someone with one Jewish parent and one parent from another blood line. This certain Samaritan is Jesus. When Jesus came to the fallen man, He bandaged his wounds, pouring on oil and wine. In other words, Jesus healed our wounds of transgression. (He was wounded for our transgressions and bruised for our iniquities.) He did this by pouring on the wounds the oil (Holy Spirit) and the wine (His sacrificial blood). Then He took the man to an inn, leaving the man in the ministering hands of the Church. The next day, He gave the innkeeper two denarii (a form of money) and asked him to take care of the man until He returned.

It is important to note the two denarii given as payment because they give us insight about when Jesus will return for us. Although this concept is discussed in the end of times chapter, another explanation in light of Jesus' words is warranted. In Jesus' parable of the workers in the vineyard, the workers were paid a denarius for one day of work. This indicates that the certain Samaritan (Jesus) was planning to return to the man in two days. However, in God's system, a day is like a thousand years, and a thousand years are like a day. Therefore, we can surmise that Jesus will return approximately 2,000 years after He left. Folks, I don't know about you, but my calendar indicates that we are living in these days! Jesus' second coming and the end times draw nigh.

What exactly is God waiting on? The Lord is not slow in keeping His promise, as some understand slowness. He is patient, not wanting anyone to perish, but wanting everyone to come to repentance. He is waiting on the Church to minister the gospel to the people so that they will be cured of their fatal wounds of transgression and be ready for eternal life with Him.

Chapter 9
MAKE A CHOICE

God Chose Us

God chose us. He chose us before the creation of the world to be holy and blameless in His sight. He predestined us to be adopted as His sons through Jesus Christ, in accordance with His pleasure, and will to bring all things in Heaven and on earth together.

God made known to us the mystery of His will, which He purposed in Christ. Praise to the Father, Who has blessed us in the heavenly realms with every spiritual blessing in Lord Jesus Christ. In Him through His blood, we have redemption and the forgiveness of sins.

Will You Choose Him?

Multitudes, multitudes in the valley of decision! For the day of the Lord *is* near in this valley. Everyone will be judged according to and against His Word. So, we know what we are going to be held accountable for. The criteria for judgment should not be surprising. Our loving God gave us all the information we need in His Word. All we have to do is read it and apply it.

The Law of the Ten Commandments states the following:

THE BIG PICTURE

1. You shall have no other gods before me.
2. You shall not make for yourself or worship an idol.
3. You shall not misuse the name of the Lord your God.
4. Remember the Sabbath day by keeping it holy.
5. Honor your father and your mother.
6. You shall not murder.
7. You shall not commit adultery.
8. You shall not steal.
9. You shall not lie.
10. You shall not covet your neighbor's house.

Have you ever told a lie? What does that make you? Have you ever taken anything that was not yours? What does that make you? Have you ever looked at someone lustfully? What does that make you?

Chances are you are a liar, a thief, and a fornicator, among other things. If you died this very instant and you hadn't accepted and confessed to Jesus Christ as your Savior, you would be judged and cast in the fiery pit for eternity. It does not matter how holy you are, or think you are. The *only* way to escape Hell and live eternally in Heaven is through the blood of Jesus.

Jesus told the Pharisee, Nicodemus, that the only way you can enter the Kingdom of God is to be born again. The only way to escape death is to be born again, and the only way to be born again is to accept new life through Jesus Christ. For God so loved the world that He gave His only begotten Son, that whoever believes in Him should not perish but have everlasting life.

If you are washed clean in the blood of Jesus, have put on His white robe of righteousness, and have been redeemed by Him, you will be found without sin in the presence of the Lord and will spend eternity in Heaven.

We are living on borrowed time. Every day is a gift from the Creator. But the day of the Lord will come like a thief. **Make a choice!** And beware; by *not* making a choice, you are in fact *not* choosing Jesus. If you choose life in Christ, pray aloud this simple prayer:

Dear Heavenly Father,

I accept Jesus Christ as my savior and redeemer. I believe He died for my sins. I ask that my sins be forgiven and that I'm washed clean in His blood. I confess that He is Lord and I will live my life serving Him. Amen.

If you prayed this prayer, or have ever prayed a similar prayer, take comfort. Look forward to the day of God because in keeping with His promise are promised a new heaven and a new earth, the home of righteousness. Make every effort to be found spotless, blameless, and at peace with Him. Be on your guard so that you may not be carried away by the error of lawless men and fall from your secure position. Grow in the grace and knowledge of our Lord and Savior, Jesus Christ.

Amen.

ABOUT THE AUTHOR

BEYR REYES received her doctorate degree in Biomedical Science. She has over 200 publications in science, medicine, and Christian genres. She has spent the last several years teaching and mentoring Christian writers, and even started ShadeTree Publishing to provide a more accessible publishing venue for them and to serve as a birthing station for their careers. In addition, she has worked in the drug industry since 2005 as a regulatory writer for major international pharmaceutical and biotech companies. (Beyr Reyes is Jennifer Minigh's penname for the Christian genre.)

You can contact Beyr Reyes via email, Twitter, or Facebook:

Beyr.Reyes@ShadeTreePublishing.com

@JenniferMinigh

Facebook.com/Jennifer.Minigh

All of Dr. Reyes' proceeds from this book will be given to the Kingdom of God.

OTHER BOOKS BY BEYR REYES

489: a short story about forgiveness

Loaded with plot twists and surprises, this short story delivers a powerful message about forgiveness and how our life affects other people, even those we don't know. The book is widely endorsed by therapists and ministry leaders because it helps the reader to be set free from the bondage of unforgiveness.

Your Write Calling: Is Writing Right for You?

Have you been toying with the idea of becoming a writer? If so, this book is for you. Learn what it means, and what it takes, to be a Christian writer. After reading this book, you will understand what the call to write looks like. In addition, you will know how to get equipped and what to write. The book, which is endorsed by Jerry B. Jenkins, contains soul-searching questions to help you decide all along the way.

Fast Answers:
When You Need Answers Now

Other fasting books tell you why to fast or explain the importance thereof, but leave you guessing how to even start. This book puts legs on your intentions so that you can walk it out. "Fast Answers" has mapped fasting plans with a clear starting point, destination, and goal. The plans come in one-, three-, or seven-day varieties and are tailored to specific prayer needs. No longer will you fumble your way through a fast. With this book, you will find your way to the answers you need right now. This book isn't about fast answers (as in quick ones). It's about fast answers (as in seeking God ones).

Subject Your Flesh

2014 CSPA e-book of the year

Need to get control of your life? Tired of constant dieting? Fed up with bad habits? Subjection is the answer that lasts. Learn how to eradicate the problem areas in your life. Take control of your flesh and turn your life around using the Word of God.

Make a Choice
2011 Readers Favorite Silver Award

This book is a continuum of revelation designed to challenge your foundational beliefs and then challenge you to stand on those beliefs. In Unit 1 (Choose Your Beliefs), you will ask yourself questions like: Is God really God? Is Jesus God? Is the Bible true? In Unit 2 (Live Like You Mean It), you will ask yourself: Am I really a Christian? Am I really saved? Am I really forgiven? All along the way, you will make decisions that will affect your life forever.

THE BIG PICTURE

ACKNOWLEDGEMENTS

This book is a synopsis of God's Word. I pray it is an acceptable sacrifice unto Him.

Thanks to David and Julia for lending their time and thoughts so that I could write this book.

Thanks to Gary and Karen Parham for opening my mind to the Big Picture and for their wonderful editorial comments.

Thanks to April Reynolds for her insight and wonderful editorial skills.

Thanks to Linda Morris for her instruction, encouragement, and most of all, prayers.

Thanks to Dee Kroeck for her encouragement and exhortation in completing this book.

REVIEW REQUEST

I hope you have gained some insight about the Bible and God's master plan.

Now that you've read this book, if you enjoyed it, then please let other readers know. Let's share the knowledge and help people grow in the Word and the Lord.

/ THE BIG PICTURE

REFERENCES

1 Mark 10:8-9
2 Gen 1:26
3 Gen 1:28
4 Gen 1:29
5 Gen 2:16-17
6 Gen 3:1
7 Gen 3:4
8 The American Heritage® Dictionary of the English Language (4th Edition, 2000)
9 Job 9:33
10 Job 33:24
11 Job 16:19
12 Job 19:25
13 Is 59:20
14 Gen 9:1
15 Gen 9:11 and Gen 9:13
16 Gen 12:2
17 Gen 17:9
18 Exo 24:8
19 Jer 31:33
20 Note: The only reference in the Hebrew Bible that uses the wording "new covenant" is Jeremiah 31:31-34.
21 John 1:32-34
22 John 20:22
23 Luke 24:49
24 John 12:31
25 John 7:37
26 Cutshall B. *Unlocking the Prophecy Code: Understanding Bible Mysteries in Types and Shadows*. Pathway Press: Cleveland, TN; 2005.
27 Matt 23:39 and Luke 13:35
28 Matt 24:4-5
29 Griffith W. *Israel's messianic Jews: some call it a miracle*. CBNnews. 2008.
30 Human Development Report 2007/2008: Economic performance in GDP per capita annual growth rate
31 Rev 5:5 NIV
32 Rev 7:9-10
33 Rev 7:14-17
34 Rev. 11:15 NKJV
35 Rev 14:6-11
36 Rev. 14:15 NIV
37 Lev 26:18
38 Lev 26:21
39 Lev 26:23-24
40 Lev 26:27-28
41 John 7:37-38
42 Jer 31:31
43 Cutshall B. *Unlocking the Prophecy Code: Understanding Bible Mysteries in Types and Shadows*. Pathway Press: Cleveland, TN; 2005.

www.ingramcontent.com/pod-product-compliance
Lightning Source LLC
LaVergne TN
LVHW041642060526
838200LV00040B/1677